CW01494544

This book is dedicated
to the memory of all soldiers
who served in The Great War

CALENDRIER POUR 1918

PREMIER TRIMESTRE

JANVIER
FÉVRIER
MARS

DEUXIÈME TRIMESTRE

AVRIL
MAI
JUIN

TROISIÈME TRIMESTRE

JUILLET
AOUT
SEPTEMBRE

QUATRIÈME TRIMESTRE

OCTOBRE
NOVEMBRE
DECEMBRE

Robert B. Ela
Co.A 29th Engineers
A.E.F.

AGENDA

DU

COMMERCE

DE L'INDUSTRIE

ET

DES BESOINS JOURNALIERS

1918

Robert Blazo Ela (Pa)

Introduction

My grandfather Robert Blazo Ela (or Pa as we called him) was a lovely man.

I was ten when he died in 1960 so I can remember a hard-working, gentle, fun, quiet man who loved his family and could beat anyone, bar my Nana, at cribbage.

I discovered that I owned his precious diary while looking for something to take to an Antiques Roadshow filming day. I was touched and delighted to read of his World War I experiences in France and decided to put the diary into book form in order to share it with my siblings and cousins. His story is a common one but as my publisher pointed out no one had looked into this book in almost one hundred years ... this is unreconstructed, honest history and should be shared.

The daily entries of this diary are faithfully reproduced. Any occasional misspellings, punctuation errors or lapses, strange use of capital letters, nonsequiturs, or random odd letters/numbers are what he wrote. I have tidied up his syntax on very few occasions to ensure that his entries make sense; he was an educated man so I am sure he would have done the same if time and circumstances had permitted. His opinions and prejudices are his own and are of his time. His sense of humor escapes me but how comforting to know he laughed while 3,500 miles away from home and living with strangers in a war zone.

What factual information I was able to find is included in the appendix. We have a copy of his June 1st, 1917 Draft Registration form from York, Maine but because US Army records from 1912 to 1959 were destroyed in a terrible fire in 1973 his service record is unavailable. Also, the archives of the cantonment of Camp Devens have no extant record of the thousands of young men trained there before being shipped overseas. We do, however, have photos of Camp Devens from the time my grandfather would have passed through on his way to "somewhere in France."

Family provided a copy of some German propaganda as well as a photo with a hand-lettered label indicating that Pa was still in Europe in 1919. The National Personal Records Centre, part of the National Archives held in St. Louis, Missouri, has provided a copy of his final discharge financial settlement. This confirms a date of 4th August 1919 for his return to the States.

Shortly after his return he resumed his education and graduated cum laude from the Bromfield Pearson School at Tufts College in Massachusetts with a Bachelor of Science in Mechanical Engineering awarded at Commencement on June 21st 1920. His transcript reveals a much improved attention to learning after the war.

He married my Nana, Mary Alberta Martin (the Berta of his diary) and had four children: my Uncle Bob, my Dad Charles (aka Chick), my Aunt Ruth and my Uncle David. He lived and worked for as long as I knew him in Worcester, Massachusetts.

The genealogical information about Pa came as a complete surprise to me. I had always assumed that the Ela name was of European origin but had been butchered and/or shortened by well-meaning but possibly semi-literate staff at Ellis Island in the early twentieth century. What a treat to discover colonial beginnings for both the Blazos and the Elas!

What have I learned about the man himself while transcribing his words and thoughts? He seems polite and kind but realistic about his fellow soldiers. He is organized enough to make a diary entry nearly every day for almost a year. He is well-read and most observant of his surroundings. He can describe a sunset almost poetically but worries a lot about his chow. The fact that the original diary has the page of each date divided off and 1919's day and date pencilled in may indicate that he is the tiniest bit tight-fisted. Or perhaps, since he has no idea when the war might end, he just wants to be prepared and is optimistic about his chances of survival. He has an exceptionally generous Uncle Waldo and a somewhat mysterious relative called Gertrude Ela who may or may not have had a run-in with a censor.

Pa was not a war hero. His was a quietish war. He writes without fanfare of surviving behind the lines as a carpenter, map maker, blueprint technician and draughtsman. Although he writes of no feats of outstanding valour or heroism I'd like to believe he was a very brave and loyal soldier as well as a steadfast son of New England who didn't made a fuss. I am very proud of him.

Nancy J. Ela Hearley

Janvier

1 MARDI Circoncision 1-364

"King Alcohol" a venerable bird that made the trip with us from S-N-, kind of mascot of the company & sole survivor of our Thanksgiving feast. Rather noisy early in the morning. Just at present... he needs a bath. His principle hangout is in the kitchen on the wood pile.

We also had a little white "chien" but whether we had him for dinner or whether he just got lost somewhere in France we will never know. He is now among the missing.

The army has its good and bad sides.

It certainly puts a man in fine physical shape and teaches him many valuable things.

On the other hand it makes a sort of "crab" out of some fellows. If they can't find something to "crab" about they are never happy. The principle but for all discontent is the grub. We have been feeding so good that when the eats fall a little below the standard you hear the "crabs" holler.

Some fellows sit and talk like a couple of kids when they get into an argument. They may grow up someday?

Janvier

2 MERCREDI St Basile 2-363

One of the fellows in the kitchen name is Frank. He is a married man and has children. The other day, one of the fellows, who was sort of financially embarrassed, went into the kitchen, and asked this fellow if he had 5 francs. This fellow said sure, if you want to go and get it. The other fellow was all smiles and said "Where is it. Back in the States replied Frank. And he was right. He has a wife and 4 little Franks back home.

"King Alcohol" certainly makes a good guard. His post is in the kitchen. Well we have quite a lot of rats in the kitchen, that like to frisk around the kitchen at night. We have a trap and some mornings have four or five of the vermin. Well Old King Alcohol will get in front of the trap and when one of the rats sticks his nose out through the bars of the trap he will take a peck at the rat.

Janvier

3 JEUDI St Geneviève   3-362

You hear many funny incidents that happen between the natives & the "Sommies." Many of the natives don't understand English. The café proprietor in the following incident did not. When you go into a store and ask for something that they are out of they will say "finish." Well one night one of the fellows went down to this café and asked for some "pommes de terre." "Finish pommes de terre," replied the proprietor. The fellow by this time getting a little out of patience asked for some beef steak. "Finish boeuf-stec" replied the proprietor. When the fellow heard this he lost his patience entirely and said in a very disgusted voice "Jesus Christ." The keeper thinking that was something more to eat replied "Finish Jesus Christ."

Janvier

4 VENDREDI St Rigobert   4-361

Janvier

5 SAMEDI Ste Emilie   5-360

Went on guard as supernumery
  " down town with 2 prisoners, weather very cold.
  " out to the gate from 9:30 to 11P.M.
Guard house very smoky (not much sleep.)

Janvier

6 DIMANCHE Epiphanie   6-359

Went down town A.M. Prisoners
Came off guard at 12:20.
Mail came.
Letters from. Berta & Lila & Ruth McHale, Aunt Annie
14 bundles papers from Uncle Waldo.
Box from Berta (S.S. Pierce) Christmas fine condition
*   " " Stoneham Church   " " "*
Weather very cold and windy
When I came back from town could hear church bells ringing. It sounded very pretty.

Janvier

7 LUNDI Ste Mélanie   7-358

Received letter from Lila in regard to box sent by Dean Class.
Wrote to Aunt Annie & to Ma.
Weather: - Snowy.
Went on hike this morning. Rather slippery walking.
Wrote to Berta.

Janvier

8 MARDI St Lucien   8-357

Went on guard down town. Had very comfortable quarters. Q.M. (1st relief.)
Weather snow & cold.

Janvier

9 MERCREDI St Julien   9-356

Met Donald Fowle at 8:30A.M. He is with 101st Engineers. He invited me to supper.

Came off guard at 1P.M.
Went down town after retreat and took supper with Donald A. Fowle.
Had a fine time. Met another fellow in 101st Engineers. It was very snowy.
Arrived back at camp about 7:30P.M.

Janvier

10 JEUDI St Guillaume   10-355

Went on guard 12:20 at gate (3rd relief)
Weather cold and snowy.

Janvier

11 VENDREDI St Théodose   11-354

Came off guard at 1 P.M.
Still snowing
Washed clothes in afternoon.
Had a letter from J. McHale 101st M.P.

Janvier

12 SAMEDI St Arcadius   12-353

Pay Day (for Nov. & Dec.) Rcd.   167.00 franc
                          Haircut   1.00
                          Balance   166.00
Weather:- Rain along toward night.
Moved the office.
Inspection.
Water supply cut off. (supper)? bread, syrup & coffee.

Janvier

13 DIMANCHE Bap. de J.-C.   13-352

Rain & Snow all day. Very sloppy.
On detail in morning.
Went down town after retreat & bought a few things.

Made box for one of the fellows.
Washed and read some of the papers Uncle Waldo sent.
Souvenirs that some of the fellows bought.
Received 5 francs from J. J. White (loan).
Quite a crowd down town in evening.
Bought battery for flashlight.

Janvier

14 LUNDI St Hilaire   14-351

Bright & Fair. Prospects of a very fine day. Rather rough walking.
Went down town and bought a few belated Christmas presents.
Wrote to Aunt Annie & Berta.
Bought a pipe over at the commissary.
New moon last night. Fine night.
Little lunch (Bread & Karo) at 3:00 P.M.
Can buy sugar, canned stuff tobacco & Karo syrup over at the commissary.
Prices very reasonable. (Sugar 7 1/2 cents American money)
Can also get oleo. 23¢.

Janvier

15 MARDI St Maur   15-350

Rain & Windy. Rather chilly all day.
Had indoor work all day.
Went down town to-night. I got a few more souveners to send back to the folks.
Chief indoor sport chess. Some pretty warm contests. Made the board to-night.
And this is sunny France???
A year from now "the wrath on the Rhine" will be an Ingersoll according to
J. J. White.
Made hot chocolate over the canned heat. Real cow's milk!! Delicious!!!
Time to go to bed. 9:35 Good night.

Janvier

16 MERCREDI St Marcel   16-349

7 A.M. Rainy and very windy. Snow going pretty fast.
12 Noon: Rain stopped but wind still holds. Went on hike this morning and the
walking reminded me of part of Tennyson's poem "The Brook"

I slip, I slide, I gloom, I glance,
But never on the ground.
For the officer may be around.
I splash through puddles galore
And wonder if there are any more.
For rain may come and rain may go
But we march on forever.

Sun tried to poke out thru the clouds; no success.
Went down town after retreat. Pretty sloppy.
Wrote to Jim McHale 101st M.P. Co.B.

Janvier

17 JEUDI St Antoine   17-348

Windy and a little rain A.M.
Snow most all gone. Don't think it will last very much longer.
Sun came out for a short time about noon.
Made a small box to send things home in. Must pack things up and send them along.
Saw several French soldiers with their girls to-night when I was down town.
French store keepers much different from American. Not so business like.
Must write to Ma.
No Mail as yet.
This is a great crowd to argue. No matter what the subject & you don't have to know anything about what you are talking about. Just argue. The fellow who can talk the fastest wins.
Got a half pound of oleo to-day.

Janvier

18 VENDREDI Ch de S.P.   18-347

Cloudy and cool A.M. Tried hard to rain but without success.
Had two bundles of papers from Uncle Waldo to-day. They were dated right around Thanksgiving time. Sunday Herald & Boston Traveller. Dated Nov. 29th.
Sent away a box of souveners to the folks at home. Addressed it to Berta. Hope they receive it in good condition. Postage 1, 40 francs. Deposited 2 francs for Postage.

Feeling fine. Cold all gone.
The snow is nearly all gone.
To-night it is trying to rain. Rather misty.
Am going to be real domesticated to-night and stay in and read & write.
Nothing out of the ordinary happened to-day. I guess the only news is, B- is sober. First time since payday.
The chessers are at it again but don't think there will be any blood spilt.
Am going to write a short letter to Berta.
Have a little spiritual entertainment to-night.

Janvier

19 SAMEDI St Sulpice   *19-346*

7 A.M. Cloudy and very windy
Later:- the sun came out and if it was not for the wind it would have been nice and warm.
Had inspection and went on hike. The roads were rather muddy but not so very bad. The country was very pretty. It looked like spring. The grass seemed to be about ready to turn green and the snow was all gone except for a few small patches in sheltered spots.
This being a half holiday the boys in our room thought they would try their hand at domestic science. They made some taffy.
Recipe:- Karo quantity unknown, sugar also unknown quantity, & small piece of butter (oleo) 1st batch came out fairly well (could have boiled it a little longer.) Used our stove and w. pan, mess kits. 2nd batch (too many cooks.) One part came out well so that we had hard candy to-night.
Got some pictures of our wanderings to-day. They were very good. (2 Francs.)
Went down town to-night. There seemed to be more light in stores than usual.
Military funeral to-day. Makes you feel kind of funny when you hear the band playing.
Still no mail.

7 A.M. Fair and very windy. Temp. about 50°F.

Had physical drill this morning and then were off for the rest of the day. Hung around the barracks until dinner. Had steak, potatoes, bread & coffee.

About 1 o'clock, Chrysler, Bowers & I went for a walk out to the cave. It was very windy and we took it head on all the way out. It was about 2 ¹/₂ miles (4 kilometers) out there. Bowers took a camera and we took some pictures. I hope they come out good. There is a history that goes with this cave:- It seems that sometime about 65 A.D. a certain Roman, named Sabinus conceived the idea of founding a kingdom here, with himself as head. He journeyed here and started his project with fair success at first. He ruled with an iron hand & a wooden head, I guess, for the people rose up. Sabinus, in order to save his neck, fled with his wife, Epionne, to this cave, overlooking the valley where the Marne River rises. Here, he and his wife lived in peace (except for family squabbles) for 9 years, when the Romans came and took Sabinus to Rome where he lost his head (literally.) Exit Sabinus 78 A.D.

The cave is not very extensive. Sabinus & his frau could not have been very prolific as they would have to sought a larger tenement. There is one large room & a den leading off the main room. There are 2 entrances to the main room. It would not do to be in the habit of walking in his sleep as he might wake up in the valley.

The valley of the Marne is very pretty. The snow is all gone and the grass is beginning to sprout. The fields are all plowed up and ready for planting. The roads are in fine condition.

To-day some of the boys made some more taffy. It was pretty good but not cooked quite enough. We could eat it without any trouble.

It is funny that you find some fellows that don't know how to help themselves. 9 o'clock time to turn in.

Janvier

Fair and warm all day. Temp. about 50°F.

Was carpenter to-day.

Went down town after retreat. The days are getting longer but I hope the cold weather does not return.

No mail. Am afraid it has shared the fate of the Lusitania as we are due for mail again.

No matter where you go or into what walks of life you stroll you will always find some that can always find an excuse whenever they make a mistake.

Got one package of Piedmonts issued to-day. Have decided that cigarettes are very bad for the throat, especially Piedmonts. The pipe for mine or roll your own like all great men.

Janvier

22 MARDI St Vincent   22-343

Rather cloudy but pretty warm. Temp. about 50°F.

Was carpenter to-day again.

One of our carpenters sick with the mumps. There seems to be quite an epidemic of mumps just now. Well I have had them so I have not to worry about that.

This noon I got that package of laundry from Aunt Annie. I had given up any hope of seeing that laundry. Now I can change my O.D. shirt. Not that I need to as I have only worn this one 3 months.

Last night after making my entry in this book I bought some fudge from one of the fellows for $1^1/_4$ francs. He made it and it was fine.

Got two bundles of papers from Uncle Waldo this afternoon. One bundle of Times Nov. 15th-17th. Sunday Herald (Nov. 18th, 1918.)

Wrote to Aunt Annie & Uncle Waldo.

Had an air raid scare about 6 P.M. It was all over in about half an hour.

Had a shower to-night at retreat. It was all over before 6 o'clock.

Janvier

23 MERCREDI St Raymond   23-342

7A.M. Rather cloudy but fairly warm.

Had a shower about 10 o'clock and another one this afternoon about 4 o'clock. It has been a sort of open & shut day to-day. The sun would come out and then it would cloud up again.

Worked all day as a carpenter. No matter what you say you can't beat the things that come from the U.S. Take tools for an example. We have some French tools and some U.S. tools. You can feel the difference just picking them up. We had some lumber that came from Miss. U.S.A. It looked like lumber. Had to work overtime to-night unloading lumber. Went down town after I finished

work. I must be getting pretty poor as I was only saluted once. Well the days are getting longer and it is lighter later. Another case of mumps to-day.
Nice moon to-night but it is rather cloudy.
No mail to-day.

Janvier

24 JEUDI St Timothée   24-341

Fair & Warm. Temp. about 50°F.
Was a carpenter to-day the same as yesterday.
Feeling fine. This is the kind of weather that gives a fellow the spring fever.
Went down town this evening after retreat. It was pretty light. The moon was out so that you could see nearly as well as daytime.
Another beautiful sunset to-night.
No mail to-day.
Wrote to Berta to-day.

Janvier

25 VENDREDI Conversion St Paul   25-340

Rather foggy all day but fairly warm. Temp. about 45°F.
Was a carpenter some more and expect to remain as such for some time to come.
To-day was a BIG DAY. MAIL.
Both first class mail & packages.
My list of mail was as follows:- Postcards from; Berta (2), Mrs. Weed, Miss Connor. Letters from:- Aunt Annie (2), Berta (2), Walter, Ma, R. Parker, Wagbourne, Beth, E.B. Roberts, Lil McKenzie; Packages from Uncle Waldo No 4 (I think) & small box from Lila part of the lot that was sent from church. Letter from "Kid." Now I have some job on my hands to answer this mail.
Made a small table over in the carpenter shop. We had a bunch of lumber came in the other day and it works fine. It came from U.S.
To-night after supper we all read our mail over again and then had a sing in our room and then one of the fellows borrowed a harmonica and played until after 10 P.M.
The fog lifted about 8 o'clock and the moon and stars came out. Fine night.

26 SAMEDI Ste Paule   26-339

Cloudy or rather foggy all day Temp. about 45°F.
Still on the job as wood butcher. Am working on 8 small tables. Some job. There is work enough to last for some time.
We had another batch of packages to-day. I had a bundle of papers from Uncle Waldo. Record dated Dec. 7, 1917.
I must get my mail in shape and maybe write a few letters before I turn in.
There was a band out on the parade ground this afternoon and they certainly did sound fine.
Chief indoor sport just at present is making toast & cocoa over our little stove in the barracks.
To-morrow we have inspection
About 9 o'clock the fog lifted and the moon and stars came out bright.
Well it is 10:30 so I must turn in.

Janvier

27 DIMANCHE Septuagésime   27-338

7 A.M. A slight mist this morning. Not very cold but rather damp.
9 A.M. Inspection; Personal & Barracks.
10:30 Sun out and nice and warm. The boys are out playing ball and enjoying themselves in general.
I got caught laughing at inspection this morning, so expect to do K.P. or follow the "ponies" for a couple of days. Cause:- Kid Bowers bottle of syrup put us all in good spirits.
Note to "Bob" Parker, Walter, & Beth this afternoon. The sunset to-night was very beautiful. There was a heavy bank of fog in the west which looked like a large lake. When the sun sank there were some soft fleecy clouds that were painted a vivid hue or rather various hues from bright red to the deepest purple.
I wrote a letter to E.B. Roberts to-night.
Well it is 8:30 and I am going to turn in.
Oh yes, I nearly forgot, we had steak & pie for dinner to-day.
More spiritual entertainment this evening. Leading man S---R.

Janvier

Fair and warm. Temp. about 40°F.

This morning when we stood reveille the moon was shinning in the west and the sun was just coming up in the east. It was a very pretty sight.

Acted as carpenter to-day.

This noon had some more mail. As follows:- 2 letters from Berta, 2 from Aunt Annie, 2 from Tufts Club, 1 from Gertrude Ela, 1 from "Demps," 1 from Jim and Mary. In one of Berta's letter were some pictures, taken last summer. It seemed good to see the folks again.

Had another beautiful sunset to-night.

Got some candles over at the commissary. 7 for 10 cents American money.

Wrote to Jim MacDonald.

Sent address card to Tufts Club.

Moon got nearly full. Very pretty; nice and clear.

Janvier

7 A.M. Fair and cool. Temp. about 40°F.

Had another very pretty sunrise this morning.

12:15 Very warm and sunny out. Regular April day. Had another job handed me this morning. From the extent of the job we will be busy for at least a week. Carpenter work, making shelves; a whole room full of them. I am getting to be a regular carpenter. Must write a few letters and get caught up with my correspondence.

There was a little mail this morning but I did not have any. Maybe I will have some again. Just at present I have enough mail to last for some time.

I wrote a 5 page letter to Gertrude Ela.

Moon got full to-night. (I don't know if it was cognac, or light wine.)

9:00 P.M. must turn in.

Janvier

Fair and cool. Temp. about 38°F.
The sun was out nice warm at noon.
To-night we sign the payroll and to-morrow we have muster.
That job I am on will be good for a month at least. When we get that done I don't know what we will get next. I like this carpenter work.
It has been a fine day but rather cool. Another beautiful sunset to-night.
I must write some more letters to-night. I have six to write to fix up my correspondence.
We signed the payroll for January to-night.
Wrote to "Kid" Ellis
Went down town about 7 P.M.

Janvier

6:30 A.M. Foggy and rather cool this morning
Still on the carpenter job.
This noon I received box #1 from Uncle Waldo. I guess the things are coming all O.K. now.
6:30 P.M. It is still foggy and chilly.
Got five bundles of papers from Uncle Waldo.
Wrote to Aunt Annie.

Fevrier

7 A.M. Foggy and rather chilly. Temp. about 40°F. Worked on same job to-day. This noon when we went in for dinner I saw a very pretty and at the same time odd sight. The trees around the parade grounds were all covered with a very heavy frost. When the sun came out it melted just enough so that each tree had its own individual snowstorm. The ground under each tree was all white.

Wrote to Ma to-night.

One of the fellows (P.K. Bunn from Kansas) sprung a good one to-day. A couple of the fellows were having an argument on how to pronounce a certain word. P.K. spoke up and asked how do you pronounce P-E-R-U-N-A. One of the fellows spoke up and said Peruna. (He swallowed hook, line, and sinker.) P.K. then replied "Doctors pronounce it harmless.

Another fellow got off a good one the other night. It seems that according to the Good Book the war is to end on 22nd of February. This fellow said that if the war did end then he would join the church. (Tuttle)

Received the following from Ma:

A CREED

I will be true, for there are those who trust me;
I will be pure, for there are those who care;
I will be strong, for there is much to suffer;
I will be brave, for there is much to dare;
I will be a friend to all the poor and friendless;
I will be giving and forget the gift;
I will be humble, for I know my weakness;
I will look up, and laugh, and love, and lift.

Fevrier

Fair and cool 7 A.M.
This noon was nice and warm. It certainly was a fine day. It was so nice and warm this noon, that it seemed too bad to go to work inside this afternoon. Same job as yesterday.
To-night we had another beautiful sunset. I went down town to-night after supper.
Wrote to Berta this evening.
To-day was Ground Hog Day.
No Mail to-day.

Fevrier

Sunday:- Fair and warm.
It certainly was a fine day.
We had inspection this morning and I got away in good style.
This noon we had blackberry jam pie. It was fine but you had to work fast to get outside of it as it was rather juicy.
I went down town this afternoon after dinner. I guess everyone was out. It certainly was a fine day. The road was full of them.
Wrote to Wagbourne to-night
No Mail to-day.
To-night Carl Renard and I bunked "ensemble." He was going out on detatched service early in the morning so he rolled his pack to-night.

Fevrier

7 A.M. Cloudy but warm.
Sometime during the night we had a shower and it was pretty muddy this morning.
10 A.M. Sun came out, and it was nice and warm. This noon there was a notice on the bulletin board making me a carpenter until further notice.
Went down town this evening after retreat. The roads were pretty muddy.
No Mail to-day.

It is pretty quiet here this evening. Frank Dunnington from Washington D.C. is away. Also P.K. Bunn with his dry Kansas humor. Shaver and Lord are both out somewhere and I expect Glasgow is down town learning a little more French. "Kid" Bowers is also away.

Fevrier

5 MARDI Ste Agathe   36-329

7 A.M. Kind of cool, but fair.
The sun came out and we certainly did have a fine day. Nice and warm. On the same job again to-day. This noon we had mail. I had a letter from Ma and Box #6 from Uncle Waldo & Co. That certainly was a fine vest that Berta sent. When I went over after my box, the skipper was in the office and he said (in stage whisper) "You had better go over to the Hospital and get some pills."
This afternoon we had more mail. I had a letter from Berta, Aunt Annie, Preston, and a small diary from Uncle Waldo. I also received a cartoon of Camel Cigarettes from Lil McKenzie.
At mess formation (5 P.M.) there was an announcement that there would be a special formation at 7 P.M. It sounds like pay, to me. Sure thing to the tune of 83.50 Francs.
Saw them breaking some saddle horses this afternoon. Some sight. Also saw a Scotch Kiltie to-night. He certainly did look odd.
Don't feel like writing to-night.

Fevrier

6 MERCREDI Ste Dorothée   37-328

Cloudy & damp all day. warm
About 5 P.M. it rained.
This morning I had 9 bundles of papers from Uncle Waldo. The latest date was December 31, 1917.
Was on the same job to-day.
Went over to the commissary to-night and got some candles, butter (oleo), and lemon drops. They have a good stock in over there. Camel cigarettes 2 pkg's for 11 ¢.
Don't feel like writing to-night.

Fevrier

7 A.M. Cloudy but fairly warm.
Same job again to-day.
The sun came out for a little while this afternoon.
Janitor J.J. White appeared to-day with his "sergeant's chevrons" (crossed brooms), this noon.
Job is not going very well. Expect more success to-morrow.
Had another bundle of papers from Uncle Waldo, this noon.
Have just finished a book entitled "Nonsense Novels." Very good. By Stephen Leacock
Wrote to Dempsey
* "   "   Preston*
* "   "   Lil McKenzie.*
One of the fellows pulled another good one to-night. (Roby). We were talking about killing animals and to cap the climax (R-) said that he knew a man who used to kill hens by wringing their necks. He said this fellow was giving a demonstration on a rooster. R- said he twisted said rooster's head around about 3 times and then set him down. All the rooster did was untwine his neck and walk off. That broke up the party.

Fevrier

7 A.M. Cloudy & showery little chilly.
We had flapjacks for breakfast. Very good.
12 Noon. Sun out nice and warm.
No Mail to-day.
Boys out to-day tossing the "pill" around. Looks like spring. The days are growing longer.
Wrote to Russell Leavitt
* "   "   Berta.*

Fevrier

7 A.M. Cloudy and damp.
This morning every man in the company received a Red Cross bag. They were
not all the same. In mine I got a towel, toothbrush & paste, a bar of highly scented
toilet soap, a couple of pair of shoestrings (leather) a can of Velvet tobacco, 4 bags
of Bull Durham, 2 packages of Lucky Strike cigarettes, and 2 pkgs of ZigZag
cigarette papers.
On the same job to-day.
Had a letter from Aunt Annie this noon (dated Jan 11th,)
A little problem in mental arithmetic. Two farmers both having chickens met on
the road and during the conversation number 1 asked No.2 how many chickens
he had. He told him a certain number. Then No.2 asked No.1 the same question
and No.1 told him. Well No.1 said to No.2, you give me one of your chickens
and I will have twice as many chickens as you. No, said No.2, you give me one of
yours, and we will both have the same number.
Question:-How many chickens did each farmer have? [Ans No.1- 7 No.2 - 5]

Fevrier

Fair and warm. Temp. 50°F.
Had inspection this morning after which I took a walk down town, and took my
laundry down.
Wrote to Aunt Annie & Uncle Waldo.
Wrote to Ma this afternoon
Went down town again after retreat.
We had a very brilliant sunset to-night.
Heard another good one to-day. There was once upon a time, a widow who had
two sons. Now these two sons wishing to gather a few more shekels to their
worldly possessions bought a cattle ranch. Now most of these ranches go by some
name. What should they call their newly acquired ranch was the question. Their
mother being of a facetious turn of mind suggested they call it "Focus." When
some one inquired the significance of this name, she replied. Why focus is the
place where the sun's rays meet.
No Mail!

Fevrier

7 A.M. "Brite" and Fair.
It certainly was a fine day to-day. Warm and sunny. To-night we had another beautiful sunset.
Worked on the same job to-day. It begins to look like something now.
Just at present a bunch of the fellows are around the stove having a sing. They get a little harmony once in a while.
Three months ago to-morrow we hit "sunny" France. How the time has flown.
Wrote to P. A. Carr to-night.
No Mail to-day.

Fevrier

"Brite" and Fair Very warm. Temp. about 55°F.
Worked at my same job making shelves to-day.
Had a letter from A.S. Waldron 101st Engineers Co. C. He wrote that he is going to take his 7 day leave soon. I hope he comes this way as I would like to see him. [Answered letter to-day.]
To-day is Lincoln's Birthday but not a holiday as we expected. I think we will get our holiday next Saturday.
We had cake for supper to-night.
We had mail to-day; mostly packages. I had two boxes from Uncle Waldo & Co. And a can of maple sugar from K.A. Potter.
In one of the boxes was tobacco (2 cans), cookies, candy, stationary. In the other, cookies, cake, candy, jacknife, and stationary.
There was a very interesting article in the Jan 5th Saturday Evening Post entitled "Hitting Our Stride in France." It is very true to life in this country at the present time.
Had a very warm argument on Art to-night.
Had 8 bundles of papers from Uncle Waldo and one bundle of papers (Post Jan 17, 1918.) (sender unknown.)

Fevrier

Fair and warm (kind of cool this morning.) 7 A.M. It came off rainy about 10 A.M. and was wet all day.
I was working on the same job to-day.
Had a bundle of papers from Uncle Waldo.
Wrote to Katherine Potter to-night
* "   "   Jim McHale   "   "*
* "   "   Gertrude Ela   "   "   (censor?)*
Had a regular "sing" to-night.
To-day I gave one of the fellows some of those cookies that she sent. He thinking to be facetious said "I could kiss the girl that made these." I told him that I would have to refer him to my aunt."
Another little pathetic story.
"She laid the little white form down gently and then.....cackled."

Fevrier

6:45 A.M. Wet and drizzly. Kind of cool. And to-day is St. Valentine day. I wonder if I will receive any valentines.
This has certainly been a busy day. We worked making mess tables. They are made on the same plan as those at Camp Devens. We made 24 of them to-day. Some days work.
There was one on the bulletin board to-night. We hear quite a little about Washington D.C. and how it is considered the best city in U.S. Well in the supplement of one of the Sunday papers there was a picture showing five little pickaninies seated on a bench. Under the picture it said, "They still live in Washington D.C. There was another picture showing a very sleepy recruit being aroused from his slumbers at a very early hour. Well we have a fellow from Washington D.C. who upholds his home "town" on every occassion. He is very fond of sleeping so as he somewhat resembled the sleeping beauty we put his name underneath it and it soon appeared on the bulletin board.
Had a bundle of papers from Uncle Waldo.
Wrote to Walter
* "   "   Beth*

Fevrier

15 VENDREDI St Faustin   46-319

Kind of cool this morning but it came off nice and warm this noon.
Worked at my regular trade to-day, making benches for the major. Some job.
It was rather cool all day to-day.
Made a bunk for Bert Chrysler to-day. I hope it don't break down.
No mail to-night.
Wrote to Berta to-night.

Fevrier

16 SAMEDI Ste Julienne   47-318

Fair and cold (br---r.)
It was certainly cold to-day. This morning there was ice about half an inch thick
on a pail of water outside the kitchen door. The wind was very sharp. We noticed
it more because we have had such nice warm weather.
Worked at the same job to-day. We had a half holiday to-day. There was a sort of
meet but our company did not show up very well. Reason:- lack of training. I was
in the tug-of-war but we were beaten.
I gave my vest its first tryout to-day. It certainly is fine.
Made myself a bunk to-day. I am going to christen it to-night.
Went down town to-night after retreat. Very quaint ideas over here. Saw the
postman to-night. His dress resembles very much like that of the French soldiers.
He carries the mail in a small leather bag. To-night he carried a small square
lantern.

Fevrier

17 DIMANCHE Quadragésime   48-317

Sunday:- Pretty cold but fair.
Had inspection this morning.
My new bunk certainly did feel fine last night.
Wrote to Aunt Annie & Uncle Waldo.
*   "   "   Lila.*
Air raid scare. Nice bright moonlight night. Clear as a bell and cool.
Some fellows who are supposed to have some sense fail to show it. They act like
kids when it comes to an argument.
No Mail.

Fevrier

Fair and cool, this morning. Mackinaws felt very good.

Have another boil. This time under my left arm. Am going over to the hospital and have it opened up. Went over to the hospital to see about my boil. It was under my left arm and not any too pleasant. I had it opened and let the matter out. The doctor was very good. He introduced a little "Ethel" to me. "Ethel" is a very cold personage; her last name being Chloride; but she certainly did ease the pain. Now I am as good as new. Oh yes, I had a little shave thrown in (under the arm). No Mail.

Wrote to Ma to-night.

We were playing cards to-night on our new table and I had on my leather vest and had my hat tilted back on my head and was smoking my pipe I must have been an odd looking sight; or at least one of the fellows said, "You look just like a sheep herder."

Fevrier

Fair and cool Temp. about 30°F.

Worked on same job to-day.

To-day we had mail. I had a letter from Berta, one from Lila, and one from Aunt Annie. In Lila's letter were some pictures.

One of the fellows had a pie on his shelf and he was sitting at the table facing the shelf, so that no one would "borrow" it. Well he got playing cards and in the mean time someone "lifted" the pie from the shelf. Well I got blamed for the job. In the other room they had a "little roughhouse." They broke up several bunks and found one fellow asleep and moved him bed and all out into the hallway. They claim that he was slightly enebriated, but I doubt it very much. Once in a while we do have fellows that come in and are very much like fleas "Full of Hops."

Subscribed for the "Stars and Stripes Three months for 4 Francs. A weekly paper.

Fevrier

"Brite" and Fair. Cool Temp. about 35°F.

To-day had it fairly easy. Worked in the morning. In the afternoon took a nap and about 3 P.M. took a trip down to the station in an auto-truck. It was certainly some pretty sight, as we were going down the long hill. The valley lay, spread out before us. We visited a saw mill. They are certainly way behind the times when it comes to machinery.

Went down town to-night after retreat and got my laundry. It was only 1.10 francs and I had an O.D. shirt, 3 towels, 3 handkerchiefs, and a pair of stockings. Cheap at half the price.

To-night saw some children playing a game which very much resembles our game of hop-scotch. The "kids" over here are regular beggars.

No Mail to-day.

Wrote to Berta.

Fevrier

Cold and rainy all day.

When we got up this morning, the ground was covered with a light blanket of snow. But it started to rain and the snow disappeared rapidly. It was very disagreeable out. I worked outside in the rain, picking out lumber at a French sawmill. In France you don't see much soft wood. It is all hard and that which we get is all hard, green and very heavy. The methods they use for sawing lumber "over here" are much different from ours. I saw one saw that was rigged up like a vertical hack-saw. The blade, or saw worked up and down by means of a large eccentric; the blade being supported by a frame that ran on vertical ways. Another machine was a circular saw, not very large and the log had to be fed into the saw by hand. I also saw several large canal boats. This was very interesting as I once read a French story entitled "La Belle Nivernaise," and these boats reminded me of that story very much. In this mill they don't saw any lumber over 12 feet long, because the logs are so crooked. We rode back and forth to work in a car (I mean a Ford truck.) When I got back from work, I found that we had mail. I had letters from Berta, Lila, Aunt Annie (no.16), Beth and P. Goding. I had a package of tobacco from the Tufts Club. Also 3 boxes from Uncle Waldo & Co. In these boxes were the following articles:- toilet kit, scarf, working gloves, figs, tobacco, gum, handkerchiefs, cigars, hard candy, cookies, chocolate, bullion cubes and towel. I also had a box of pills from Aunt Annie. It was great fun opening the boxes and I think the other fellows enjoyed it as much as I did. In Berta's letter there were some more pictures. Also in Berta's letter was a picture of my nephew, Dick.

Fevrier

22 VENDREDI Ste Isabelle   53-312

Washington's birthday: Nothing to do but work.
Cold & cloudy in forenoon, rainy & cool in afternoon.
Worked down at the mill all day.
This noon we had mail. I had 4 copies of "Life" from Berta, 4 bundles of papers from Uncle Waldo & 1 bundle of Saturday Evening Posts from Ma.
Saw some Algerian soldiers, and they were certainly a motly looking crowd. I think that they had been up to the front.

Fevrier

23 SAMEDI St Mérault   54-311

Rainy all day. Very disagreeable.
Worked all day as carpenter.
After retreat went down town. Very muddy walking. Opened up a new YMCA. They had movies, the first I had seen since I left the States, that is real American pictures. Then after the pictures, they gave us an apple apiece. These apples came from Washington State. They also served hot chocolate, but I did not stay for it as it was getting late.
Visited No.1 to-night, merely a tour of investigation.
No Mail to-day.

Fevrier

24 DIMANCHE Reminiscere   55-310

Cloudy all day. Had inspection this morning. Nothing to do but lay around for the rest of the day. Had pie for dinner.
Wrote to Tufts Club.
   "   "   Ma
   "   "   Beth & Will.
No Mail to-day.

Fevrier

25 LUNDI St Gothard   *56-309*

Rainy and disagreeable all day. Worked at my "trade" again to-day.
This noon we had more mail. I had letters from Aunt Annie and from Ma. Box
No. 12 from Uncle Waldo & Co. and three bundles of papers from Uncle Waldo.
Wrote to Aunt Annie.
    " "   Berta.

Fevrier

26 MARDI St Nestor   *57-308*

Fair and Cool. The sun came out and we certainly had a fine day.
Worked to-day making bunks.
This noon we had mail. I had a nice long letter from Berta.
We had a very pretty sunset to-night. A pink and red one.
I also got 2 bundles of papers from Uncle Waldo.
Fine nice bright moon light night.

Fevrier

27 MERCREDI Ste Honorine   *58-307*

Cool and rainy all day.
Worked all day making bunks. Some job.
Had a letter from Russell.
Wrote to Gertrude Ela.

Fevrier

28 JEUDI St Théophile   *59-306*

Rainy in A.M. Started to snow about 5 P.M. & it snowed all night.
Had muster this morning; also inspection. The skipper thought my shave was
rather old.
Worked all day making bunks; wireing them up. It was certainly some job and I
was glad when 5 o'clock arrived.
After supper we went over and signed the payroll for February.
No Mail.

A funny little incident happened the other day. We were unloading some stuff off a truck and there were some boxes about 18" long and 6" square. Well, these boxes were pretty heavy, (about 175 pounds.) They called one of the fellows to take the box in. He came out and seeing the size of the box grabbed hold of it as though it was a box of feathers. Well, I'll bet his fingerprints are still on the box. He tried to put it on his shoulder but "nothing doing." He finally managed to get the box in, but not until he made some struggle. Maybe we didn't laugh at him.

Stars and Stripes Forever

Mars

1 VENDREDI Ste Eudoxie   60-305

Rainy nearly all day. The ground was all white when we got up this morning.
Worked all day wiring bunks.
This noon we had mail. I received 3 letters from Aunt Annie, 2 from Berta, 1 from Ma, and 1 from Jim.
Must answer some mail.

Mars

2 SAMEDI St Simplice   61-304

Snowy all day. Not very cold.
Worked all morning wireing bunks. Hope we finish them to-day. Finished bunks.
Wired up 17 to-day.
Wrote to Walter this noon.
*   "   "   Berta to-night.*

Mars

3 DIMANCHE Oculi   62-303

Fair and Warm. The sun came out and the snow melted pretty rapidly.
Had inspection this morning.
After inspection took my laundry down town. The roads were very muddy.
Had a letter from Phil Carr.
Had pie for dinner.
After supper went down to the "Y." They had a service, and it was very good.
Wrote to Phil Carr.
First issue of the Stars and Stripes came out to-day.

Mars

4 LUNDI St Casimir   63-302

Snowy all day. I should say that we have had about 6" so far.
Feeling kind of rocky all day. Stomach out of order. Layed around the barracks all
day. Am feeling much better this evening.
Wrote to Ma
* "   "   Aunt Annie*
No Mail

Mars

5 MARDI St Adrien   64-301

7 A.M. Brite & Fair. Am feeling fine this morning. Worked on shelving job all
day.
About 9 P.M. it started to snow and snowed until after dinner.
We had mail to-day. I had a letter from Ma, and one from Aunt Annie (#20). In
Aunt Annie's letter was a letter from Pa and a short note from Berta. Her guess
was not very far off.

Mars

6 MERCREDI Ste Collette   65-300

"Brite" & Fair Warm.
Snow going very rapidly. Rather slushy and muddy but we are well equipped
with rubber boots so we keep our feet dry.
Worked all day as a carpenter.
Wrote to Lila and Berta.
No Mail to-day.

Mars

7 JEUDI Mi-Carême   66-299

"Brite" & Fair Foggy in the morning.
Worked all day making more bunks.
We had "slum" for supper. Rather watery. The boys didn't care much for the feed
and they had quite a little talk about it.
After supper three of us took a walk down town. I got a battery for my flashlight

and then we went in and had some hot chocolate. Then we went up to the "Y."
They had a sort of stunt night. Had boxing and some of the bouts were very good.
They had one fellow who had a very peculiar movement. He worked his right arm
just the same as a grasshopper moves his hind legs. It was very funny. We got
some cookies, and then we came home.
No Mail.

Mars

8 VENDREDI St Jean-de-Dieu   67-298

7 A.M. Cloudy and it is trying to snow this morning.
Had flapjacks for breakfast. They made one of the fellows, who made quite a holler
about the supper last night, a big flapjack. I think it was fully 18" in diameter.
Worked all day as a carpenter.
The sun finally came out and we had an ideal day overhead altho somewhat
muddy underfoot.
Saw about 5 flying machines to-day. The "woods" was full of them.
No Mail to-day.
Wrote to Russell.

Mars

9 SAMEDI Ste Françoise   68-297

Brite and Fair. It was certainly a fine day. Nice and warm. All the fellows had the
spring fever. Worked all day as a carpenter making window frames.
This afternoon went over and took a nice warm bath. I have a very nice cold.
My voice is leaving me. To-night we get paid for February about 8:30 to-night
[received 83.50 Francs.]
To-night we lose an hour's sleep. They set the clocks in France & England ahead
that hour to save daylight. So we lose some sleep to-night.
Had mail to-day. Letters from Aunt Annie (#17), Jim McHale, and a card from
Uncle Waldo.
Our esteemed corporal from Washington D.C. is minus one mustache. He made
the rather foolish assertion that one of the fellows couldn't take it off. Result:-
The bunch got hold of him, threw him upon a bunk and cut off said mustache.
The operation was a successful one in more ways than one.
Then when one of the fellows went to bed, he found that someone had lined his
bed with various articles, such as rocks, boards, iron, and an old hand grenade. I
got blamed for the job but I swear I am innocent.

Mars

"Brite" and Fair. Nice and warm.
Had inspection this morning. Then we were off for the rest of the day. Took some laundry down town and got the batch I took last week (1 Franc) After dinner went down town again. We took a walk and then a couple of us had our pictures taken. They will be finished next Sunday. Hope they will be good. We had some fun while they were being taken. Came back to the barracks and took a nap.
Don't like this idea of moving the clocks ahead one hour. We don't have retreat until 5:55 now.
I have "some" cold. My voice sounds like a file. My throat is not sore however.
Yesterday I picked up a small hand grenade. It was not loaded and I am using it for a candle stick.
No Mail
Wrote to Aunt Annie
    " "   Berta.

Mars

Brite & Fair.
Was under the weather to-day. Went over to the hospital and got some medicine. Came back and had a haircut.
Didn't work all day. Just layed around all day.
It certainly was a fine day nice and warm.
No Mail

Mars

Brite & Fair. Very warm, fine day.
Felt better this morning. Went to work. Was on mess hall detail to-day. And worked as a carpenter all day.
Went to bed early.
Sent copy of "Stars and Stripes" to Aunt Annie.
No Mail.
Had electric lights to-night in the barracks. They are fine.

Mars

Brite & Fair. Fine day; nice and warm.
Worked all day as a carpenter
This noon we had mail. I had a letter from E.B. Roberts, one from Aunt Annie, and one from Berta. In Berta's letter there was a picture of herself.
After retreat 3 of us went down town and took supper. We had 3 fried eggs apiece, (trois oeufs), bread and butter (du pain et du beurre), French fried potatoes (pommes de terre), and chocolate (same word). All this for 3 francs. (51 cents). The eggs are cooked in small earthenware dishes and served in the same dish. The supper was very good. We came back to the barracks and I am about to write some letters.
Am feeling a good deal better to-day.
Wrote to E.B. Roberts.

Mars

"Brite and Fair." Fine day to-day. Nice and warm.
Worked all day as a carpenter.
You should have seen "Old King Alcohol" to-day. One of the fellows held a mirror up in front of him and he immediately got indignant at the "other" rooster and was ready for a fight. He ruffled all up and tried to put the other rooster out of business.
We had mail to-day. I had a letter from Bernice and one from Walter.
Wrote to Walter
   " " Bernice
   " " Ma.

Mars

Fair and cool this morning. It was cloudy all day and pretty cool.
Worked all day on carpenter detail.
This noon we had more mail. I had a letter from Berta and one from Aunt Annie (#19). In Berta's letter she made another guess; very close this time.
To-day we had two issues of the "Stars and Stripes."
My cold is better.

Wrote to Berta
Sent 2 copies of Stars and Stripes to Berta.

Mars

16 SAMEDI St Cyriaque   *75-290*

"Brite and Fair." Fine day.
Cold is much better.
Worked all day on the carpenter detail.
After supper we went down to the "Y." They had a very good show on. There
were several quartettes from the different companys. There was a big crowd down
there. In fact all we could get was standing room. The quartettes were very good,
but the star performer was "Elsie Janis," an American actress; she was very good
telling stories and singing songs. There was such a crowd that I could not hear
what was going on. So we went outside in back of the stage and we could hear
everything, but we could not see what was going on. She sang a song entitled
"Over Here." It goes something like this:

Over here, Over here.
Send the word we are here
We all are working, no one is shirking.
Mother dear, dry your tear
Soon this war will all disappear.
We're glad we're over, we're glad we're over
And we won't be back, until it's over over here.

She also sang "Your Country and My Country." After she sang it herself, she
sang it like some other people would sing it, such as Ethel Barrymore, Harry
Lauder and other singers. Some of her stories were very good. One about a
colored man who wouldn't enlist.
I did not stay for the entire performance. We came back to the barracks.
One of the fellows sprung a good one to-night. He is always springing something
new altho some of them wouldn't look well in print. Well we were talking about
dogs and remarked that we had not seen many dachhounds. This fellow spoke up
and said you mean the kind you pat on the head and he wags his tail <u>ten minutes</u>
later.
No mail to-day.

Mars

17 DIMANCHE La Passion St Patrick   76-289

Brite and Fair. Fine nice sunny day.
Had inspection this morning.
After inspection went down town and got my laundry and my pictures. The
pictures came out better than I expected.
"Old King Alcohol" appeared this morning with a nice green ribbon around his
neck. He didn't seem to like it very well.
Went down town to-night and had supper.
Wrote to Aunt Annie & Uncle Waldo (2 pictures)
    "   "   Berta (2 pictures)
No Mail

Mars

18 LUNDI St Alexandre   77-288

Brite and Fair.
Worked all day on carpenters detail.
No Mail
Wrote to Ma (2 pictures)

Mars

19 MARDI St Joseph   78-287

Cloudy all day.
Worked on carpenter work
Turned in our ponchos and got a slicker.
Rained about 4 P.M. and rained all night.
After retreat five of us went down town and had supper. Had fried eggs, French
fried potatoes, bread, butter, and chocolate, also jam.
No Mail
Had steak and mashed potatoes for dinner.

Mars

Rainy all day. Kind of cool.
Worked all day on carpentering work.
Had a regular Irish dinner to-day corned-beef and cabbage.
No Mail

Mars

Cloudy most all day. The sun would come out once in a while.
Was under the weather this morning. Did not work. My stomach was not behaving just right. I must have eaten something that went against the grain. Slept most all the morning. Worked this afternoon on the powerhouse.
After supper Bert and I went down to the "Y." It was not very muddy walking. There was a very beautiful sunset to-night. The whole western sky was lit up bright red and shading off to pink, then a blue and finally the light was lost in a dark purple.
No Mail to-day.
Wrote to Beth.
To-day according to the reports in the papers the "Boche" started a big offensive along a fifty mile front.

Mars

Brite and Fair. Nice day.
Worked on carpenter detail all day.
The third issue of The Stars and Stripes came out to-day. It was a very good issue.
Went down town after supper. There was not anything much doing.
No Mail
The British are holding the Germans but both sides are suffering heavy losses. The British having the advantage. About forty German divisions were used in the offensive.

Mars

82-283

"Brite and fair." It certainly was a fine day. Nice and warm.
Worked on power house detail. This army life is certainly a lazy life. I don't know why it is, but you seem to lose all your ambition. Everything is regulated and you get into a sort of machine-like regularity and you don't have to think for yourself. If this war lasts too long I will be so lazy that I won't be worth my salt, when I get back to the States.
Sent my third copy of the Stars and Stripes to Ma.
Bert "my bunkie" has gone away so I will have to seek other company until he returns.
Last night after supper I took a trip down town. Place was pretty quiet, but there was a big crowd down at the "Y."
No Mail to-day.
The sun when it went down was certainly beautiful. It was just a big red ball of fire and it gradually disappeared below the horizon like a big cheese sliding down behind a shelf.
The battle on the front is still going on.

Mars

83-282

Brite and fair. Another nice warm day.
Had inspection in the morning and then I took some laundry down town. Stopped at the "Y" and got some cigarettes.
This afternoon after dinner I went out in back on a nice sunny slope and wrote a letter to Jim and Mary. Then I went to sleep in the sun.
To-night I wrote to Berta.
Got a bundle of papers from Uncle Waldo.

Mars

84-281

"Brite" and Fair. Nice warm day.
Worked on carpenter detail all day.

This noon we had mail. I had six bundles of papers from Uncle Waldo and box No. 13 from Uncle Waldo & Co. There was a camera, rolls, candle, tobacco, chocolate and writing paper. There was no first class mail.

Mars

26 MARDI. St Emmanuel   85-280

"Brite and Fair" Rather chilly all day. This noon we had a little flurry of snow. Worked all day on the carpentering detail.
No Mail to-day.
Wrote to Aunt Annie & Uncle Waldo [2 pictures.]

Mars

27 MERCREDI St Ruppert   86-279

"Brite and Fair" Still fairly cool.
Worked on the same job to-day making tanks for the photographic room. Some job!!!
To-night we had mail. I had a letter from Aunt Annie (#24), a card from Berta, a letter from the Tufts Club, and a letter from H.N. Shepherd. In Aunt Annie's letter was a short note from Berta.
Wrote to Tufts Club.
*   "   " Ma.*
Was a show here last night. A Mr. & Mrs. Richardson entertained. They say it was very good. They told several good stories. Here is one about a Jewish fellow, that was standing guard. Some one approached his post and the following conversation took place.
Guard:- Halt!!! Who is there?
Voice:- Friend.
Guard:- Advance and give the discount.
Another one about a very consenscious Frenchman who was trying to learn the English language. He practised on every occasion; and one time when he thought he had bothered his teacher quite a little, he offered the following apology. "I am very sorry if I have cockroached on your time." The teacher told him he meant encroach not cockroach.
"Oh, yes," replied the Frenchman, "I always did get those genders mixed."

Mars

28 JEUDI St Gontran 87-278

Brite and Fair Weather much the same as yesterday.
Worked on the same job to-day. Feeling pretty tired to-night.
No Mail to-day.

Mars

29 VENDREDI St Jonas Good Friday 88-277

Cloudy and Rainy all day. Fairly cool.
Worked on carpenter detail all day.
This afternoon we had mail. I had two letters from Aunt Annie, 1 from Berta, 1
from Walter, 1 from Gertrude Ela, and one from Katherine Potter.
Yesterday I was making some boxes and I got one of the end pieces a little short.
The "boss" came around and noticed the defect on the box and wanted to know
how that happened. Without thinking what I was saying I replied, "Why, I cut
that piece too short on one end." I didn't even smile and I don't think the boss
caught on to what I was saying.
To-day we received another issue of the "Stars and Stripes."
Wrote to Gertrude Ela
Received a box of shoe polish from Uncle Waldo.

Mars

30 SAMEDI St Amédée 89-276

Cloudy and rainy all day. Very disagreeable day.
Worked all day on carpenter detail.
This noon I received a fountain pen from Uncle Waldo. It works fine. This being
a sample of what it will do.
Wrote to Aunt Annie & Uncle Waldo.
*   "   "   Berta.*

Mars

31 DIMANCHE Paques Easter 90-275

To-day is Easter but a very poor one. It rained nearly all day. We did not have
inspection until 1:30 P.M. I went down town in the morning and got some

44

laundry. It was pretty wet out. When I came back I wrote some letters. I wrote to Walter, Katherine Potter, and Lila.

We had inspection and muster at 1:30. After that we signed the payroll for March.

After retreat five of us went down town and had supper. We had four fried eggs apiece, French fried potatoes and bread and butter. It was a very good feed and only cost us 2 francs and 7 cents.

Then we dropped in at the "Y" and got some chocolate.

Bert came back to-day and he certainly had some trip. He got me a book of views of the place where we first went after we landed in this country.

They certainly have strange customs in this country. Take the Railroads for example. When you ride on the trains in this country, you don't buy a ticket, you pay when you get off the train.

Avril

Rainy all day. Very disagreeable day.
Worked on carpenter detail all day.
This noon I had a bundle of papers from Uncle Waldo. Also a copy of the Tufts Weekly.
To-night we had mail. I had a letter from Ma, one from Dempsey, 1 from Lila, 1 from Berta, 1 from Aunt Annie. In Aunt Annie's letter were those pictures I sent for.
Sent my last copy of the Stars and Stripes to Aunt Annie.

Avril

Rainy most all day.
Worked all day on carpenter detail. Made a gutter.
About 4 P.M. it cleared off and we had a very pretty sunset in fact it was beautiful. The clouds were banked in the west and when the sun went down a flaming ball of fire these clouds were all colored up with very vivid colors. It was so beautiful that words can not describe it.
No Mail to-day.
Wrote to Jim McHale to-night.
*   "   "   Shepherd.*
You hear a bunch of very witty remarks in our squad room. Usually there is bunch of them just after taps every night when we are getting settled in our bunks for the night. There was a good one last night. One of the fellows (J. J. White) is from "Worchester" and he remarked how the express train used to wake him up every night. One of the fellows wanted to know if he slept in the freightyard.

Avril

3 MERCREDI St Richard 93-272

"Brite" and fair most all day. It clouded up this afternoon.
Worked on carpenter detail most all day (Making tanks.)
This noon I went over and got weighed on some American scales. I was somewhat surprised when I found that I weighed 185 Ibs. I had on my "blues"
To-night we got mail. I had a letter from Aunt Annie, one from Walter and one from Dempsey.
Bet made to-night between Donnington and Love (stakes 1 sou apiece). Love bet that we would not be in the States by Christmas 1918. Same bet and stakes between Love and Jones. Bowers bet Roberts 4 sous against 2 sous that we would be home by Christmas 1918.
I am stakeholder. Total 0.50 francs.
Wrote to Dempsey.

Avril

4 JEUDI St Isidore 94-271

Cloudy all day.
Worked on carpenter detail all day.
There was mail this noon. I had a letter from Ma one from Aunt Annie and one from Jim Harrison.
Was going to write some letters but did not feel like it.

Avril

5 VENDREDI St Vincent 95-270

"Brite" and fair nearly all day.
This morning went down town and took my first lesson in gas masks. Got a French and English mask. Didn't mind the gas. All we got was "tear" gas. All it made you do was to make your eyes water. One of the fellows remarked this noon at mess that a gas mask was a big improvement on Glasgow.
This noon we had mail. All packages and papers. I had four bundles of papers from Uncle Waldo and a box of goodies from Uncle Waldo & Co. In the box were some "mouchoirs," candy, rolls, & tobacco.
This afternoon I worked on carpenter detail.
To-night went over and took a bath.

When I opened my box I put my things in back of me on my bunk. Well one of the fellows took a box of candy when I wasn't looking. Well after I got all my things unpacked I noticed it, but did not say a word. After awhile the fellow pulled the box out from under his pillow and said, "Look what the folks sent me." He opened it up and handed it to me. I asked him if it would be all right to pass it around.

Avril

6 SAMEDI St Célestin   96-269

Cloudy all day.
Worked on carpenter detail all day.
This afternoon we had mail. I had a letter from Aunt Annie and one from "Kid" Ellis. Kid's address is [E.O.C.N.A U.S. Arsenal, Watertown, Mass.]
The skipper sprung a good one to-night at retreat. He is a very ardent advocate of temperance and in fact of the three things that are ruinous to mankind, the only one that is permitted in this company is "Song". Well we got paid to-night and the skipper gave us a little lecture. He said, I want you to remember that wine, women, and other drinks are prohibited in this company.
Received 82.50 francs.

Avril

7 DIMANCHE Quasimodo   97-268

Rainy most all day.
Had inspection in the morning and took some laundry down town. Pretty rainy out.
Wrote to Aunt Annie & Uncle Waldo.
*   "   "   Berta & Lila.*
*   "   "   Phil Carr (2 pictures.)*
Nothing unusual happened to-day.
No Mail
Wrote to Jim Harrison

Avril

8 LUNDI St Albert   98-267

Rainy all day.
Worked on carpenter detail all day.
This noon we had mail. I had a letter from Berta and box No.1 from Uncle Waldo
& Co. It was sent on the 9th of November and came through in fair condition.
A box of Christmas candy looked like a brick of harlequin ice cream. However it
tasted good and is all gone to-night. Then to-night I received a package of tobacco
from the Tufts Club.
Wrote to Tufts Club.
Had a letter from Berta containing 3 pictures, a calendar, and a short letter from
Ruth McHale.

Avril

9 MARDI Ste Marie E.   99-266

Foggy and rainy all day.
Worked on carpenter detail all day. This noon we had mail, all papers and
packages. I had 2 bundles of papers from Uncle Waldo and a copy of the Tufts
Weekly (Feb 27, 1918.)
To-night received a box from Uncle Waldo and Co. containing candy, tobacco,
powdered milk, cigars (2), cubes, and raisens.
Wrote to Ma

Avril

10 MERCREDI St Macaire   100-265

Cloudy and foggy all day.
Worked on carpenter detail all day. Put up a partition to-day.
No Mail to-day.

> *Father slipped and fell upon the ice*
> *Because he could not stand.*
> *Father saw several stars*
> *We saw our father land.*

Wrote to "Kid" Ellis.

Avril

"Brite" and fair. It seemed good to see "old sol" once again as he has been quite a stranger around these parts for the past two weeks.
Worked all day on carpenter detail:- making tables.
Had a letter from "Art" Waldron. He is in Base Hospital #66.
Got a book at the "Y" down stairs to-night

Avril

"Brite" & Fair. Another nice warm day.
Worked all day on carpenter detail. Making tables.
The grass is all green and the trees have to started to "leave" Spring is here for good I guess.
No Mail.
Wrote to Russell Frost.

Avril

Cloudy and Rainy all day
Worked on carpenter detail all day.
No Mail to-day.
Wrote to "Art" Waldron at B.H. #66.

Avril

Cloudy and rainy all day.
Had inspection in the morning and then went down town and got some laundry. Wrote some letters in the afternoon. I wrote to Aunt Annie & Uncle Waldo, Berta & Lila.
After supper we took a walk around the wall. While on our promenade we met a little French girl. She was about ten years old. She gave each one of us some

flowers and called us "camarade Americain." She was very cute. It was so foggy that we could not see much down in the valley.
No Mail to-day.

Avril

Cloudy and rainy all day.
Worked on carpenter detail all day.
No Mail

Avril

Cloudy and rainy all day.
Worked on carpenter detail all day. No; I only worked until noon. In the afternoon I went down town to learn a new process.
This noon we had mail. I had letters from Jim MacDonald, Beth, 4 from Aunt Annie, 3 from Berta.

Avril

Brite & Fair.
Went down town to work this morning. In fact we go down and back twice a day, so we have a nice walk. And just now the view of the valley is very beautiful. The grass is all green and the trees are all budded or starting to leaf out. The fields are all plowed up and ready for the spring planting. I like my new work very much.
No Mail to-day.
We were issued our "over sea" cap to-day.

Avril

Brite & Fair all day. It was a beautiful day. All the mud is dried up and the walking is fine.

Went down to work to-day.
This noon we had mail. I had letters from Ma, Aunt Annie, Berta and Lila.
Wrote to Ma.

Avril

19 VENDREDI St Léon 109-256

Brite & Fair but pretty cold. We had a flurry of snow this morning.
Went down town to work and stayed down there to dinner. We had some eggs and French fried potatoes.
The days are certainly growing longer. It is now 7:45 P.M. and the sun is just setting.
No Mail.
Issue of Stars and Stripes came out to-day.

Avril

20 SAMEDI St Théodore 110-255

Cloudy and cold all day. This noon we had a flutter of snow.
Went down town to work to-day. Same job.
No Mail to-day.

Avril

21 DIMANCHE St Anselme 111-254

Cold and snowy to-day. This noon the snow turned to rain and it was very disagreeable out.
Went down town to work this morning. Wrote to Jim MacDonald, Lila, Beth, and Berta.
After supper we went down town and had some eggs and fried potatoes.
No Mail to-day.

Avril

22 LUNDI St Opportune 112-253

Rainy all day, Fairly cool.
Went down town to work as usual. Rather muddy walking.

Have another cold.
No Mail to-day.

Avril

23 MARDI St Georges   113-252

Brite and Fair. Rather cloudy early this morning but it cleared off and was a fine day.
Went down town to work as usual.
No Mail
Wrote to Aunt Annie & Uncle Waldo.

Avril

24 MERCREDI St Gaston   114-251

Cloudy and rainy all day. Very disagreeable out. Went down town to work as usual.
When I was coming home to dinner I saw some boys playing marbles. It was a new game to me.
No Mail to-day.

Avril

25 JEUDI St Marc   115-250

Brite and fair nearly all day. This afternoon we had our first thunder shower. Went down town to work as usual. The work is very interesting. To-night we had another little shower. The sky was all clouded over and when the sun went down we could just see it thru the clouds. It was very pretty, a vivid ball of red. Heard another good one to-day. The kids over here are regular beggars. When they see you coming, they will run up to you and say, "Donnez-moi une sous" [Give me a cent.] Well one of the fellows used to "put one over" on them. When he would see a kid coming he would beat the "kid" to it and say himself, "Donnez-moi une sous pour souvenir." In most every case the kid would be so astonished that he would not know what to say. Well one day a "kid" got the best of this fellow. When this fellow met this little fellow and asked him for a sous, the little fellow surprised him and gave him a cent.
No Mail to-day.

Avril

26 VENDREDI St Clet 116-249

Brite and Fair all day.
Went down to work as usual.
To-day we had mail. I had a bundle of papers from Uncle Waldo and a copy of Tufts Weekly containing a letter I wrote to "Wag."
Had an issue of the "Stars and Stripes"
Wrote to Ma

Avril

27 SAMEDI St Frédéric 117-248

Fair and cloudy all day. But fairly warm.
Went down town to work as usual. The view of the valley was rather hazy.
It seems to be the style around here to have your hair all shaved off. There is certainly a nice bunch of "convicts" in our room.
There was a show over here a short time ago and several fellows with "short" hair sitting in the front row. The fellow who was doing the entertaining noticed them and said, "What is the idea of all these "long haired gentlemen" here this evening."
No Mail.

Avril

28 DIMANCHE St Aimé 118-247

Cloudy in A.M. Showery in P.M.
Went down town to work as usual.
Took dinner down town:- steak, F.F. potatoes and a three egg omelette. Very good.
Bought some small oranges and gave six cents apiece for them.
Wrote to Berta, A. Annie and U. Waldo.
No Mail

Avril

29 LUNDI St Robert 119-246

Foggy in the morning and cloudy in the afternoon.
Went down town to work as usual. The work did not go very well. I guess the weather conditions had something to do with it. After work I went down town and got some figs.

We had mail to-day but I didn't get any.

Avril

Foggy again this morning. Was on the mess hall detail. Went down to work as usual. It cleared off and we had a fine day up until about 4:00 when it clouded up. Signed the payroll for April.
Went down town after supper.
No Mail.

Mai

Foggy again this morning but the fog lifted and we had a nice warm day.
This morning when I went down to work I saw a sort of country fair or rather an auction sale. In an open square there were a lot of farmers who had driven in, in their rigs. From the looks I should say that it was a sort of fair, as there were horses, pigs, etc. There were also baskets in the quaint little two wheeled gigs, which contained eggs, butters and farm truck no doubt. I also saw a man who had a little stand, where he sold halters and rope. When I came back to the barracks for dinner, they were auctioning off some horses. The horses were nothing to brag about, as they were rather thin. They went thru the same procedure as they do back home at an auction sale. While I was standing there they knocked down one of the horses for 540 francs (about $94.00.) I might have given $25 for the horse. No Mail to-day.

Mai

Brite & Fair. A fine day. Went down town to work as usual. This noon we had mail. I had letters from (1) Aunt Annie, Jim Harrison (1), Ma (1), 2 cards from Berta and letter from Dr. R.H. Norton [45 Bay Street Rd. Boston.] When I came back from work at night we had more mail. I had a box from Uncle Waldo & Co containing box of candy, cigar, rolls, cookies and gum, shoe polish. I also had a package of Lowney's chocolate from Tufts Club. I also had five bundles of papers from Uncle Waldo.
We got paid to-night (83.50fr.)
Wrote to Tufts Club.

Mai

Brite and fair. This morning the bugler was not on the job. Therefore several of the fellows including me overslept. The "Skipper" came up thru the barracks and caught us in bed. Went down town to work as usual. When we came back from work we found that the "Top Cutter" had a long list of names of those who needed an application of yeast to get them up in the morning. This list was read at retreat and I was one of the "sons of rest." We were told to form outside the barracks at 6:45 P.M. We expected to have to drill for an hour but were happily disappointed. The "Skipper" just talked to us and advised us to purchase an alarm clock if we could not wake up on time, and then dismissed us.
No Mail to-day.
Wrote to Jim Harrison & Ma.

Sheldon S. Roby awoke one morn
And found that he'd missed reveille's horn.
Hearing someone at the foot of his bed,
Like a Jack-in-the-box, he raised his head.
There was the "Skipper," pencil in hand
Taking down names to beat the band.
One look was enough for this bold lad,
Who knew that he was surely in bad.
Like a snail drawing into his shell,
Roby dove under the covers, quicker than h-l.

Mai

Brite and Fair Another nice warm day. Everybody was on deck for reveille this morning
Went down town to work as usual. It certainly was a nice day. There were a few clouds in the sky. The view of the valley was magnificent. You could see the plowed fields, the quaint little farmhouses with their red tile roofes and the roads that meander in and out and finally disappear in the distance. It is a wonderful picture and especially so when you view it just at sunset.
To-night we had more mail. I had a letter from Aunt Annie and 1 from Beth.

Mai

Cloudy and rainy all day. Went down to work as usual. Instead of going back to the barracks for dinner, two of us (Roby & I) stayed down town for dinner. We brought some bread and pear jam with us. We went down to the little café where we generally eat and had some beef steak, a three egg omolette, and some French fried potatoes. It was very good. There were some French soldiers in the café and we gave them some of our white bread. Their bread is brown and must be somewhat the same as the war bread back home.
Wrote to Dr. R.H. Norton [Tufts Club], A. Annie & U. Waldo, and Berta.
Have nothing to do after supper, I played pinochle.
No Mail.

Mai

Cloudy and rainy all day. Went down to work as usual. Had a bundle of papers from Uncle Waldo.
After supper there was a show at our "Y." A Mr. Vincent, the president of the University of Minnesota, gave a short talk. He was a very good speaker, and what he had to say made you think. After he had finished we had two real "American Ladies" entertain us. One sang and the other played the violin. They were both fine. One of the songs that she sang was "At Dawning" by Cadmun. You talk about rapid transit, well I made the record to-night. Just before she started this song I was "somewhere in France." After about a fifth of a second I was "somewhere in Stoneham," sitting on the couch with a little girl beside me and Lila was sitting at the piano singing the words to the song. Then the last song we all sang the chorus. It was "Carry me back to Old Virginia."

Mai

Cloudy in A.M. Went down town to work as usual. It cleared off about 9:00 A.M. and was nice and sunny until about 3 o'clock this afternoon when we had a thunder shower. It is still raining, and looks as though it would keep up all night. This noon I had a bundle of papers from Uncle Waldo.

Mai

Damp and rainy all day.
I was all in; guess I caught a little cold yesterday and then I ate something that did not agree with me. I went down to reveille after which I came up and crawled between the blankets. Had a couple of slices of bread for breakfast and went to bed and stayed there all day. Got up about 5 P.M. and went down and had a little supper. Felt much better.
No Mail.

Mai

Rainy most all day. Went down town to work as usual. Ate dinner down town; had the usual eggs (4) and French fried potatoes. Very good.
To-day was a holiday for the French people (Ascension Thursday.) That is when they hold their First Communion I believe. All the natives were out in their glad rags. The little girls who made their first communion were all dressed in white, with veils to match. The boys wore blue suits, white collars and black shoes. On the left sleeve of their coats, they wore a sort of white rosette. The church bells rang or rather tolled about it this noon.
It stopped raining about 5 P.M. and the sun came out and dried up some of the mud.
After supper we didn't have much to do, so ten of us went out in back of the barracks and pitched horseshoes. It was some exciting game although I will admit that our team was outclassed. We played until 8:45 P.M. or until it was too dark to see the stake. So you can see how long the days are getting.
Had a letter from "Art" Waldron.

Mai

Fair and rather misty all day.
Went down town to work as usual. Work went fine to-day.
The French mail boxes are somewhat different from ours back home. The letter goes in the same but on the outside of the box is a sort of revolving calendar with the days of the week on it. When the postman comes around on his first trip he

sets this calendar at the proper day of the week. There are also two other little discs with numbers on them, which I think are to designate the time when the mail will be collected.

To-night I had four bundles of papers from Uncle Waldo and another issue of the "Stars and Stripes."

Wrote to Gertrude Ela.

Mai

11 SAMEDI St Dagobert   131-234

Fair all day.

Instead of going down town to work I worked up here on the same sort of work. I think before long I will be leaving this place. Nothing has been said but things tend to point that way.

No Mail to-day.

Wrote to A. Annie & U. Waldo.

   "   " Lila

   "   " Berta

Mai

12 DIMANCHE St Achille Mother's Day   132-233

Rainy and cloudy all day. Very disagreeable out. Worked in the morning, same sort of work. For dinner they sprung a new one on us, in the form of carrot pie. It looked just like pumpkin pie but oh what a difference. It compared to the real thing like this 14 carrot jewelry that you buy in the 5 & 10, to the real genuine article. It was real fine rabbit food. In the afternoon I took a nap and wrote a letter to Ma.

Went down town for supper. Had a four egg omolette, fried potatoes, bread & butter.

No Mail to-day.

Mai

13 LUNDI St Servais   133-232

To-day was an open and shut day. First it would cloud up and then the sun would come out.

Worked on same job as yesterday.

To-night we had mail. I had 2 letters from A. Annie & U. Waldo, a letter and a card from Berta, and a letter from Walter.

Mai

14 MARDI St Pacôme   134-231

Cloudy all day.
Worked on the same job again to-day.
No Mail to-day.
Wrote to Walter & Beth

Mai

15 MERCREDI St Isidore   135-230

Bright and fair
Worked on same detail to-day.
After supper three of us took a walk down town. On our way we took a walk thru the park. The park is a sort of walk thru a wooded glade. The trees on both sides of the walk are very old. There are also stone benches where you can sit down and rest yourself. We saw the sunset thru the trees. It was very beautiful. We also heard some robins and other birds singing in the trees.
No Mail to-day.

Mai

16 JEUDI St Honoré   136-229

Brite and fair all day. It was a nice warm day. Worked on the same detail again to-day.
This noon we had more mail. I had 2 letters and 2 cards from Berta, 2 letters from Aunt Annie & Uncle Waldo [one of Pa's letters], a letter from Bernice, one from Walter, and a letter from Phil Carr. In one of Berta's letters there were two pictures taken down by the pond last summer.
Wrote to Phil Carr.

Mai

17 VENDREDI St Pascal   137-228

Brite and Fair. It was a beautiful day. Nice and warm just like a June day. Worked on the same job again to-day.
To-night after supper I took a walk down town and got a couple of souvenirs to send home. Wrote to Bernice and sent her a handkerchief.

No Mail to-day.

Mai

18 SAMEDI Ste Juliette   138-227

Brite & Fair. A nice warm day.
Worked on the same detail. This afternoon we had a shower but it cleared off and
we had a very pretty sunset. Worked until 9:15 P.M.
No Mail.

Mai

19 DIMANCHE Pentecôte   139-226

Brite & Fair. Another nice day.
Worked until about 10 A.M. Came up and moved. It was some job, but I finally
got settled. We just moved from one room to another.
This noon for dinner we had mashed potatoes, meat and real mince pie. It was
fine.
Wrote to Berta, A. Annie, U. Waldo, Ma and "Art" Waldron. Sent a little
souvenir to Berta.
There was some ball game to-day, between the "Hack Drivers" and the Printers.
The former were victorious to the tune of 7-3. There was a good crowd out.
No Mail

Mai

20 LUNDI St Bernadin   140-225

Brite & Fair Very warm
Worked on same detail. Had a haircut this morning. Worked until 9:45 P.M. and
it was certainly warm
No Mail

Mai

21 MARDI St Hospice   141-224

"Brite and Fair." Another very warm day.
Worked in the morning on the same detail.
After dinner I was told to report out at the garden. I went out and they put me
thru the manual of arms with a hoe. Now a hoe and I have never been on speaking

terms, so I can not say that the work was congenial. Never the less they showed me how to manipulate said hoe and turned me loose on a patch of beans. There is an old proverb in the Good Book about a sower who went out to sow [there is no mention however, of a hoer who went out to hoe.] The story goes on to say how some of the seed fell by the wayside, some fell on stony ground, etc. Well this seed in our garden fell on stony ground and sprung up with a lot of weeds. I am sorry to say that several of the beans were cut off in their youth by the ruthless hoe of the inexperienced hoer. It was some warm job with the sun beating down on our backs. But it was a change and gave us a chance to delve in the soil or rather rocks. The soil over here is very shallow and I don't see how the French farmers can raise crops that would be profitable to them. One thing sure they can't put their time as much value. However "our" garden is looking pretty well. The beans are up, the turnips have come up as thick as "cuties" on a "Dough boy's" back. The tomatoe plants have been set out, the onions looks so well that it brings tears to my eyes when I think of them. Every time I see the carrot bed, I think of that famous and newly patented 14 carrot pie that we "enjoyed" two weeks ago Sunday. The cabbage is going ahead marvellesly. The lettuce has come up but hasn't blossomed into salad as yet. We also have radishes. As yet they haven't planted the corn-beef to go with the cabbage. I understand they have taken the corn-beef seed down to one of the cafés to be "pickled." I think we will have a good crop of everything. You know the old motto:- "Spare the hoe and save the garden." The flowers are in bloom. I picked a daisy and some buttercups to-day. To-night after retreat I took a walk down town.
No Mail.

Mai

22 MERCEREDI Ste Julia   142-223

"Brite & Fair." Another nice warm day.
Was a "country gentleman" again. This "back to nature stuff" is great. I am getting to be a regular farmer.
No Mail to-day.
Saw some wild poppies in bloom.
It certainly was a nice clear day; not a cloud in the sky and just as warm as a June day back home. Saw a hawk soaring around this afternoon. Nearly every day we see areoplanes flying around.

Mai

"Brite & Fair" Another nice warm day. There was a nice breeze all day so that it was very comfortable working out on the farm. Am getting quite a burn on out in the sun. This noon we had some second class mail. I had two bundles of papers from Uncle Waldo.

At supper time we had a shower but it did not last long. It will make it much cooler sleeping to-night.

The last few days I have been eating quite a few oranges. We get them at the "Y," and they are not terribly expensive [six for a franc.]

Sent 3 copies of the Stars and Stripes to Aunt Annie & Uncle Waldo.

Mai

Brite & Fair Another nice warm day.

Having obtained my degree of B.S. in farming, I was put in the kitchen to learn a little domestic science. It brings tears to my eyes, when I think of the onions that I deprived of their outer garments. Also of the "pommes de terre" that suffered under my knife. The job cleaning pans I took "quite a shine to." Had a hard job in the afternoon removing stones from some dates [another painful operation.] And the skill that I showed in dishing out the mess. You would think that I was an old offender at the job.

The menu for the day was as follows:

Breakfast:- Rice, milk, bread & coffee

Dinner:- "Slum," bread, & coffee

Supper:- Meat pie, date pudding, bread, & coffee.

Finished up about 7 o'clock at night. Thus endeth the first day on K.P. No Mail.

Sent a copy of the "Stars and Stripes" to A. Annie.

Mai

Brite & Fair all day. It clouded up a little and the clouds seemed to frown and try to squeeze out a tear but as the song goes (every cloud has a silvery lining) and

we did not get any rain. Was on K.P. again to-day. It was about the same thing over again, the same as yesterday. The menu for to-day was as follows.
Breakfast:- Beans, buttered toast and coffee
Dinner:- Hash, bread, and coffee.
Supper:- Fried onions, "canned Willie," bread, figs and coffee.
Finished up about 7 o'clock to-night.
Washed an O.D. shirt this afternoon.
This noon we had mail. I had quite a bunch. Two letters from A. Annie & U. Waldo, a letter and card from Berta, one from Lila, one from Ma, one from Walter, one from Shepherd, one from Bert Chrysler, and a card from Russell Frost. Also a box of red pills from Aunt Annie. (Very pretty to look at.)
Another issue of the Stars and Stripes to-day. The cooks made raisen PIE for to-morrow. Somehow or other one of them got broken and we had to eat it this afternoon. (Very good)

Mai

26 DIMANCHE Trinité   146-219

Brite & Fair. Another nice warm day.
Still pursueing my course in domestic science. This is the menu for the day. Breakfast:- Oatmeal, milk, buttered toast, and coffee. Dinner:- Hamburg steak, asparagras, boiled potatoes, bread, raisen pie, and coffee [very good feed.] Supper:- Potatoe salad, "canned Willie," bread & coffee.
It was some job getting the meals and cleaning up afterwards. It is no small job to cut bread for 200 men. The bread comes in loaves about 20" long and a foot wide. Had a little shower this evening.
Wrote to Berta, Aunt Annie & Uncle Waldo, Bert Chrysler, Ma.
P.O. #729.

Mai

27 LUNDI S. Ildebert   147-218

"Brite" & Fair. Another nice warm day. I was a "kitchen mechanic" in the forenoon. After dinner I went down town to nail up some boxes. The stuff was all packed and all I had to do was nail up the cover. Finished up about 5 o'clock and came back by the way of the wall. The sky was nice and clear and there was an excellent view of the valley and the hills beyond. While we were standing there taking in the wonders of nature a train came in at the station down in the *valley and an areoplane hummed over head. The trees are all dressed in their new spring green garments; the chestnut trees have white nosegays in their buttonholes. There were also some other trees that had blossoms much the same as the chestnut only they were red. On our way back we came back thru the park. It was nice and shady.*

We had some second class mail. I had three bundles of papers from Uncle Waldo.

Mai

28 MARDI St Germain   148-217

Brite & Fair

Went down town to work. Helped load some trucks. I went to a house for some baggage. The house was of stone with a red tile roof. It set below the level of the road and about 40 feet from said road. So in order to get to it one had to go thru the garden and down a narrow flight of stone steps. The woman there evidently thought I could speak French as she sent up a heavy barrage just as soon as I showed up. At first I could not make out what she was trying to say but finally I got the drift of her monologue. It seems that she thought that the baggage was too heavy for me to carry alone. I told her in French that I would have another fellow help me with the heaviest of it. When I told her that she seemed satisfied. She had a very pretty home To be sure it was small, but it was kept neat. She had hens and rabbits in the back yard. There was also a good sized garden and a small orchard. This noon we had mail. I had letters from Walter, Aunt Annie & Uncle Waldo (2), and a letter and 3 cards from Berta. There was also a card signed "Kewpie" posted from North Station.

Wrote to Walter and Lila.

Had moving pictures to-night. They were very good.

Mai

29 MERCREDI St Maximin   149-216

Brite & Fair

Went down town to work, pasteing maps. In the afternoon I packed up a couple of boxes.

This noon we had mail, second class. I had three bundles of papers from Uncle Waldo.

Mai

"Brite" & Fair. Fine warm day. To-day is a holiday both in France & U.S. so we have had the day off. That is most of the fellows did. I had to work a short time in the morning. There was a parade in the morning down town. The stores were all decorated with French and American flags. It was a very pretty sight. The band led the parade and it certainly did sound fine. At 10:30 A.M. they went to the cemetery and decorated the graves of French and American soldiers. Everyone was out all dressed up in their Sunday clothes.

Took a nap in the afternoon and wrote a letter to Shepherd.

After supper we heard that there were going to be some boxing bouts a little ways from here, and that a truck was going out. So about 30 of us piled into the truck and went out there. It was a very pretty ride. The ring was made in a moat, there being a wooden platform with ropes around it. The position of the ring was ideal, as the crowd could sit on the top of the moat and watch the fight. There were three very good bouts, the last one being the feature and a six round affair. After the party was over we came back here. Arrived about 8 o'clock.

No Mail.

Mai

Brite and Fair. Another nice warm day.

Did nothing all day, that is no manual labor. Took a bath and packed up my things ready for my departure.

No Mail

Signed the payroll for May

Juin

Brite & Fair. Another nice warm day. To-day was our day of departure and we certainly picked out a fine one, not a cloud in the sky. We loaded our stuff onto a big English truck and it certainly made some load. Then we climbed in on top of our stuff. We were some happy bunch to get away. Anyone to see us would have thought we were going to a picnic. We have not had any rain for some time consequently the roads were very dusty, this fine powdery dust. Well we had about a sixty mile drive and you can just imagine the condition we were in. They asked me if I was a miller, also if I was going to plant potatoes in back of my ears. I was just gray from the dust and looked as tho I had jumped into the flour barrell.

We finally arrived at our destination, a small village, "somewhere in France." We were assigned to our billet and unloaded our barracks bags and stuff there. Our billet is in a house. We have three rooms, two on the second floor and one on the third floor. We sleep on bed ticks full of hay placed on the floor. I am in one of the rooms on the second floor. For light we have to resort to candles. I think that after a while we will get our billet fixed up real home like. As yet I have not had much of a chance to look the town over. It is situated on the river. They fish on the river but not with "nets." The river bends here by this town and there is a canal that runs across the bend. The canal is used as a sort of washing canal. At regular intervals there is a place where women do their washing. Also we use it to wash our faces and hands. The water runs pretty swiftly so there is no stagnant water. Another way the people get water, is from pumps situated on street corners. When we eat we line up in front of our billet and march down to mess.

The people in this town seem more friendly than the people at the last place we were. May be the reason for this is because they have not seen very many American soldiers and it is a novelty for them.

We were out last night in front of our billet, playing balls with some of the children. The old people would sit on the sidewalk and laugh and talk French to us.
We turned in about 9:30 and slept very well in our new appartments.
No Mail

Juin

2 DIMANCHE St Pothin   153-212

Brite and Fair. Another nice warm day.
Got up at 7:00 A.M. and went to breakfast. After breakfast we had some cleaning up to do over where we are going to work. We swept the floor then scrubbed, or rather washed it. Then we washed the windows and made the world look brighter. This cleaning up took us all morning. We went to dinner at noon and then in the afternoon cleaned our billet. We swept and washed the floors and made things look better in general. We finished up about 2:00 P.M. and then we were thru for the day. To-morrow we start in work.
Wrote to Aunt Annie & Uncle Waldo.
    "   "   Berta.
No Mail.

Juin

3 LUNDI Ste Clothilde   154-211

Brite & Fair Another nice day.
Worked all day getting straightened around.
After supper took a walk thru the town. The building are very old or at least they appear so. The church is of very quaint design. On one side there is an arrangement that looks like an hourglass. It is a circle and has lines running thru it some what like this and on the circumference are numbers from 1-12. Above the circle is a rod that cast a shadow on the 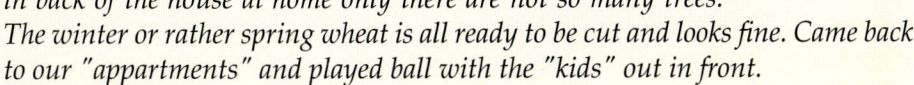 *dial. I suppose as the sun rises the shadow follows around the dial like the hands of a clock. It is very interesting. I also took a walk out by the station. The view from there reminds me of out in back of the house at home only there are not so many trees.*
The winter or rather spring wheat is all ready to be cut and looks fine. Came back to our "appartments" and played ball with the "kids" out in front.
Wrote to Ma.
No Mail.

Juin

4 MARDI Ste Emma   155-210

"Brite" & Fair. The days are nice and warm while the nights are very cool. In fact you need all three blankets in order to sleep warm.
Worked all the morning and had the afternoon to myself. Took a walk around in the afternoon. We have a Y.M.C.A. here. It is well supplied with "eats" and "smokes." They also have baseball equipment, which they let us borrow. We are planning to get our bunch together and start a ball team, just to get the exercise. You should see the women doing their washing down at the canal. All along the canal is a wall about 2 $\frac{1}{2}$ feet high. Every once in a while there is a break in the wall and there are steps where you can go down to draw water. A little further along is a wide opening in the wall and the ground right down to the edge of the water is paved with big, flat rocks. This is where the women do their washing. They kneel in a little box filled with straw and certainly make the dirt fly. The average depth of the canal is about 18 inches. There are ducks swimming around. I saw a hen with a brood of goslings and she was very much concerned because they persisted in going in the water.
No Mail

Juin

5 MERCREDI St Valérie   156-209

"Brite" & Fair. Worked all day up in our office. There was not a great deal to do. Had a letter from "Art" Waldron. He is out of hospital and on his way back to his Company.
To-night we had a show here. There were three entertainers:- An American lady who sang, a fine violinist from the Court of Roumania, and a pianist from the Conservatory of Music in Paris. It was a very good troupe. The show was given out of doors in a small park opposite the town hall. There was a wooden stage in one corner of the park and there was a natural background with the trees on the banks of the canal. The audience was a mixed one. The "boys" turned out in good numbers. And the natives from all ages between 3 and 73. The "kids" were just the same as "kids" always are. They crowded right down front and squatted on the ground. The singer sang several Indian songs one of them being "The Land of the Sky Blue Waters." The show lasted until about 9:30.
One of the fellows was saying to-day, when I asked him why he didn't save his money, that he had only one life to live. I told him he would live longer if he didn't live so fast. ["Hair Breath Harry."]

Juin

"Brite" and Fair. Nice warm day.
Worked in the morning at the office. There was not much doing in the afternoon.
All the dogs in town are muzzled. What the reason for this is I don't know unless
it is because there are so many children on the streets.
The streets here are very narrow and also very dusty. They have no sprinklers
here so everyone sprinkles in front of his own house and also have to keep the
street clean.
They also have bread cards. They are allowed so much bread a day.
No Mail to-day.

Match Problems-

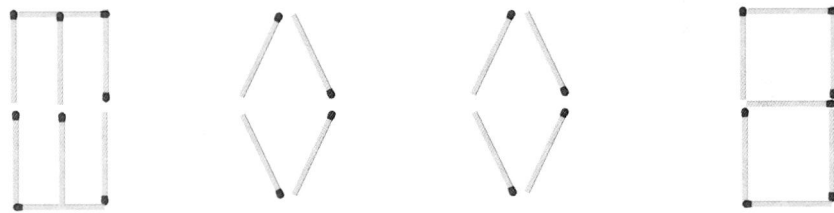

1. *Question:- Remove six (6) matches and leave what matches are made of.*
2. *Take a pile of matches [any number] and let someone draw any number of*
them from 1 to 3. Then you draw any number from 1 to 3. You keep on drawing
until the matches are all gone. The object being to make the other fellow take the
last match.

Engineers' Song (tune "Mother")
     S *is for the Soup they always hand us;*
     H *is for the Ham, we never get.*
     O *is for the Orders that they give us,*
     V *is for the Victory, you bet.*
     E *is for the End of our enlistment*
     L *is for the Last day over here.*
     Put them all to-gether, they spell "shovel"
     A tool they hand the engineer.

Juin

Brite & Fair. Cleaned up the office in the morning. Wrote to "Art" Waldron. Co.C. 101st Engineers.
You should see the donkey carts. The carts are two wheeled affairs. The donkey looks like a small pony, but he is strong and will pull quite a load.
The children here are also very cute. I saw an officer (American) go down the street and two of the little rascals, about 5 years old, stood right up and saluted just the same as we do.
Had a letter from Jim McHale.
Wrote to Beth.

Juin

Brite & Fair. Another nice warm day. Worked in the morning.
Wrote to Jim McHale
*   "   "   Russell Leavitt*
Every morning there is a little milk cart, drawn by a small donkey comes around, and the people have their pitchers or cans ready and get their milk in this way. Sometimes the little donkey will get angry and voice his sentiments in a not very musical voice. The other morning early there was a rather disgruntled donkey outside our window and he made quite a commotion. The noise woke us up and one of the fellows wanted to know what it was. One of the fellows told him it was first call.
No Mail.

Juin

Brite & Fair. Another nice day.
There was no work to do so I wrote letters in the morning. I wrote to Aunt Annie & Uncle Waldo and Berta. After dinner I had just finished a letter to Ma when someone blew assembly. We rushed out in front of our barracks and found out there was a forest fire about a mile from here. We got on our "blues" and went down to the orderly room and waited for a truck to take us to the fire. The fire was up in the hills. We finally arrived there and got the fire out. The fire burned down the side of one hill into a sort of ravine and up the other side. There was

not much to burn on the ground as the French people keep all the underbrush cleared away. It looks very neat to drive along a road and not see any underbrush among the trees. We got back from the fire about 6 o'clock and had supper. After supper we got some mail. I got two letters from A. Annie & U. Waldo, 2 from Berta, and 1 from Lila.

Juin

10 LUNDI St Landry   161-204

Fair but rather cloudy.
I awoke this morning about 4 A.M. and found that it was raining. It stopped however before it was time to get up.
To-day I am barracks orderly, you might call it chambermaid in this case. I swept our "appartment" and have nothing else to do all day, but stay here and see that nothing runs away.
Wrote to Lila
    "   "   Gertrude Ela
We got paid to-night. I drew my usual 83.50f.
Had a couple of showers to-day.
Had "movies" at the "Y."
No Mail.
Each grown person in this town is allowed 300 grams of bread a day. And each family one pound of sugar a month. Clothes are also very expensive.

Juin

11 MARDI St Barnabé   162-203

Cloudy and fairly cool all day. Nothing to do but write letters, read and sleep.
Wrote to Jim & Mary.
After supper a bunch of we engineers got to-gether and played a game of baseball against the H.Q. Troops here. The game was a seven inning affair with us on the winning end to the tune of 6-4. The scene of this great contest was on an improvised diamond on the top of the hill about a mile from camp. The diamond was in an open space on the top of the hill and was surrounded by pine trees. It was quite a climb to the top of the hill, but when you gained the summit, you were more than repaid for your efforts by the splendid view of the surrounding country. As you looked back there was the village stretched out below you with the river flowing around it. Beyond the town there was another hill about the same height as the one we were standing on. And on our left was another hill the

sides of which were all under cultivation.
No Mail.

Juin

12 MERCREDI St Guy   163-202

Brite & Fair Another nice warm day.
As we are all packed up ready for our next move, there was nothing to do to-day.
So just took it easy.
No Mail.

Juin

13 JEUDI St Antoine de P.   164-201

Brite & Fair Nice Warm day.
Nothing to do in the morning. In the afternoon we worked getting ready to move,
carrying boxes etc. About 10 P.M. the trucks arrived and we worked until about
midnight loading them. Went to bed about 12:30.
No Mail.

Juin

14 VENDREDI St Ruffin   165-200

Brite & Fair.
Got up at 4:30 A.M.; had breakfast at 5, rolled our packs, and were ready to leave
at 6. There was quite a train of trucks. The roads were very dusty. We started in
one truck but before we got out of the village it refused to go, so we had to climb
into some other trucks that were loaded with supplies. I was perched away up
on top of the load. I had a fine view from there and got out of some of the dust.
It is haying time over here and all the people are busy. Some of the fields, where
the grain has not been cut, are very pretty. In among the grain are bright red
poppies that make the fields beautiful. When we left - we were number six in
the train, but we had a little trouble so when we stopped for dinner (L), we were
last. We stopped for supper in a little village on the side of a hill (B.) They set
up the kitchen and we had something warm for supper. After supper we pushed
on again. The sun went down and the moon came up and after a while the stars
came out. We still kept on and the roads were so dusty and the roads were so
winding that as we looked back we could see a long trail of dust. After a while the
moon went down and it was as black as the ace of spades. Still we kept on. About
midnight we arrived at a town that looked like a summer place. There were large

hotels and made you think for a while that you were in some big city. We finally arrived here about 2:30 and we were some tired bunch. I was so tired that I took a walk around so I would not fall asleep standing up. The streets were deserted. The officer looked around and tried to locate some place to go. Finally about 3 A.M. we found a place to park the trucks. I was so tired that I just unrolled my pack and "flopped" right on the ground. Some one came around and woke me up around 8 o'clock. We unloaded the trucks and had some breakfast. Then we took our belongings to our billet. We are all billeted to-gether in an attic on the fifth floor. It is certainly close quarters. Worked all day down to the office getting straightened around. After supper I went to the public bath house and had a nice warm tub bath. Took a walk around town and then hit the hay.
No Mail.
Had a shower in the afternoon.

Juin

15 SAMEDI St Modeste   166-199

Juin

16 DIMANCHE St Cyr   167-198

Cloudy and rainy all day.
Took some laundry out to be washed this morning Worked at the office all day. Very busy.
After supper wrote to Berta and sent her a little birthday present. Took my wristwatch down to be fixed.
No Mail.
You hear little incidents every day. Here is one that a fellow (Sax) told on himself. When he first came over he was taking a bath in a public bath house. He had a room to himself and was comfortably located in a tub when a woman opened the door. The fellow said he only knew one word in French and that was "Entrez." And he said that was what he said.

Juin

17 LUNDI St Avit   *168-197*

Rainy all day. Rather cool.
Worked at the office all day. We are very busy.
After supper wrote to Ma. Then I took a walk around town. It is certainly some town. It was raining, but we did not mind a little thing like that. Met a French soldier that could speak English very well. Came back and went to bed. No Mail

Juin

18 MARDI Ste Marine   *169-196*

Fair but not very warm.
Worked at the office all day.
This noon we had mail. I had letters from the following:- Ma (1), Berta (1), Walter (1), A. Annie & U. Waldo (1), & "Kid" Ellis (1). It was dated previous to some mail that I got about a week ago. I also got three bundles of papers from U. Waldo.
Received another issue of the "Stars and Stripes" (June 7)
I have a slight cold in my head
Wrote to A. Annie & U. Waldo.

Juin

19 MERCREDI St Gervais S.P.   *170-195*

Cloudy and showery all day.
Worked at the office all day. We were not so very busy.
We eat in a mess hall that used to be a gymnasium. It is a dirt floor, or rather it was. Just now the floor is a sawdust one. The food is very good.
Took a walk uptown after supper to get my watch. They told me they couldn't fix it. I guess I will have to buy a new one.
We took a walk down to the station to get a paper. The daily papers come in at night on the train. It seems a very popular place down at the station just about train time. Came back and went to bed.
Had a copy of the Tufts Weekly.
No first class mail.
The gardens here are very pretty now. There is a combination flower and vegetable

garden in back of our billet and it certainly does look fine. There is a garden in the yard where our office is and that is looking fine. The potatoes are up about a foot and the other vegetables in the same proportion.
Wrote to "Kid" Ellis.

Juin

20 JEUDI St Sylvère   171-194

Cloudy and showery all day. We seem to have more rain here than we did in the last place. Maybe the reason for this is the mountains around here.
Worked at the office all day.
Had another copy of the Tufts Weekly and another bundle of papers from Uncle Waldo.
This afternoon I thought I would see what was the matter with my watch. I took it apart and found that one of the little gears that goes with the winding arrangement had a couple of teeth missing. I wound up the mainspring before I put it together and when I had it all assembled it ran OK. The only trouble is that I can't wind it up without taking it to pieces.
No Mail (1st class.)
Bought a new watch to-night. Gave 30 francs for it. I think it is a Swiss watch.

Juin

21 VENDREDI Ste Alice   172-193

Showery all day. The sun did manage to get out for a little while in the afternoon but it was between clouds.
I was working all day making blue prints for the Dorel process. As the sun was against me it was some job to get a good print. The boys certainly do "kid" one another along. They saw my copy of the Tufts Weekly and started to jolly me about being a tough guy. But a little thing don't bother me any. Another fellow (Fenton who you could always find at the little station M.s.S.) is jollied along about that. We will all be sitting around talking when some one will pipe up with, "Well I suppose when we come back to this country in about 20 years for a little visit, we will find station master F. right on the job at M.s.S".
No mail to-day.

Juin

Cloudy with local showers. Pretty cool.
Worked at the office all day. Pretty busy.
This noon we had some 2nd class mail. I had 4 bundles of papers from Uncle Waldo and a copy of the Tufts Weekly.
Had a letter from "Art" Waldron.
Read some of my papers after supper and about 9 o'clock went down to the station to get a daily paper. Came back to the barracks and "hit the hay.
You hear funny little incidents every day. Here is one "P.K." sprung to-day. He said he once knew a fellow named Buckle. His first name was Robert, so they used to call him R. Buckle. [Is not that a sweet name?]

Juin

Cloudy with local showers
To-day being Sunday we did not have to get up so early. There was no work to do at the "office" so just took it easy. Wrote to Berta in the morning. After dinner read the Sunday Herald of May 5th, and then wrote to A. Annie & U. Waldo. After supper took a walk down town and at 9 o'clock went down to the station and got a daily paper. Came back to the barracks and hit the hay.
No Mail.

Juin

Cloudy all day. With showers
Worked at the office all day.
Wrote to Ma.
After supper I read until about 9 o'clock [The Valley of the Moon by Jack London.]
Then I went down to the station and got a paper. Came back to the barracks and "hit the hay."
No Mail

Juin

25 MARDI St Prosper   176-189

Fair but it clouded up in the afternoon.
Did not do much in the morning.
Had a letter from "Art" Waldron.
About 4:30 P.M. I started making blue prints for a job. I made ten of them and
then went to supper. After supper we started in worked until about 9:30 or until
it was too dark to see. Went back to the barracks and went to bed. There were no
papers came in to-day.

Juin

26 MERCREDI St Maixent   177-188

Kind of cloudy but it cleared off about 10 o'clock. Last night I had a wonderful
dream. I was home and all the folks were there. I was having a fine time when
one of the fellows came and awoke me. I got up and got some work ready before
breakfast. After breakfast I started making blue prints but the light was pretty
poor.
Worked all day.
After supper I wrote to "Art" Waldron and then took a walk up town. About 9
o'clock I went down to the station for a newspaper. According to the papers the
Italians are giving the Austrians hell (200,000 Austrians lost.) And then there
is discention in the Austrian Parliament. Came back to the barracks and "hit the
hay."
No Mail.
Wrote to "Art" Waldron

Juin

27 JEUDI St Crescent   178-187

Cloudy and Rainy.
Worked this morning cleaning up the office. After that worked at the office all
day.
No Mail
After supper "P.K." and I took a walk. We walked out of town toward the south,
and we sure did get a fine view. There were mountains looming up that seemed
to be impregnable. We saw a farmer and his whole family out haying. The man

was cutting the grass by hand and his wife and children were raking it up. At the side of the road was a hayrack with an ox hitched in the sharves. When they would get a bunch cut and raked up they would put it on a square piece of canvass and the man would put it on his back and carry it out to the hayrack. The hand scythe that the man used was built on the same style as an American blade only the blade was wider. We saw some men over in the field so we went over to investigate. They were fishing in a sort of brook, only instead of using hooks and lines they were using their hands and wading in the brook. As I did not see them catch any fish, I don't think I will try it out. Then we walked over thru the fields to the river. We saw two men by the river, one of them fishing. When we got within talking distance we hailed them with "Bon Soir." Much to our surprise one of them spoke up and said, "I am English." The other fellow was French and he was fishing. He was catching a lot of little fish that looked some like minnows. The Englishman was a wounded soldier and had been in the hospital. He told us a lot about the war (he has been in the service since the war started) and a lot about England. The river was very pretty. I should say it was about 20 feet wide. At one place there was a very pretty little fall caused by a sort of dam that turned the water into a sluiceway and thereby to a sawmill. On our walk were also the loveliest rose trees. In one garden I saw a semi-circle of rose trees and they were all different colors. On our way back to the billet we stopped at the station and got a paper. Went to our "roost" and hit the hay.

Juin

28 VENDREDI Ste Irénée   *179-186*

Brite and Fair
Worked at the office all day. Was so interested in my work that I came back after supper and worked until about 8:30. Walked up town and got a battery for my flashlight. (I use the flashlight to read the paper by, in bed at night.) Went down to the station and got a paper. Came back to the billet and went to bed.
No Mail

Juin

29 SAMEDI St Pierre s. P.   *180-185*

Brite and Fair
Worked in the office all day.
No Mail
After supper I took a walk. We met a French soldier and he could speak English

fairly well. We walked around the town. Then we went down to the station and got a paper. When we came back to our billet we stood out in front and talked with the Frenchman until nearly 10 o'clock. While we were standing there an old Frenchman came up and greeted us. I could not get what he was saying, he talked so fast. The other Frenchman told us that the old fellow was saying how glad he was to see us in France. The old fellow was an old soldier, having seen service in 1870, and was in one of the French armies that was captured by the Germans at that time. We went up to bed and read my paper by aid of my flashlight.

Juin

30 DIMANCHE C. de S. P. 181-184

"Brite" & Fair. This being Sunday I did not arise very early. In fact, I slept so late that I missed my breakfast. Came down to the office and found a job waiting for me. I had to make a stand to hold a large case. Well two of us got at it and had it finished before dinnertime. This noon we had "beaucoup" mail. I had a letter from Ma, 1 from Dempsey, 3 from A. Annie & U. Waldo, 2 letters and 2 cards from Berta. After dinner, this being such a nice warm day, three of us decided to take a walk. It was nice and sunny, not a cloud in the sky. We walked out to the next town and around by the river. The mountains were very pretty to-day. The road lead us right around the foot of the mountain. We left the road and went over thru the fields to the river. The "natives" were all out in the fields haying. They mow and rake by hand and load the hay onto a hayrack by means of large pieces of canvass. The rack is drawn by an ox hitched into the sharves. The sharves are attached to a sort of yoke, that rests on the head of the ox. So that instead of hauling the load he really pushes it along with his head. We went over to the river and the water looked so tempting that we took off our shoes and stockings, rolled up our trousers and went in wading. The place we chose was just below a small waterfall. The water felt good altho it was pretty cool. We came out, let our feet dry off in the sun and then put on our shoes, stockings, and leggings. Then we started back for town. We figured that we were on the right side of the river, but when we got near the road, we found the river between it and us. We looked for a place to cross and finally found a place that looked pretty shallow. I told one of the fellows he ought to make it in three jumps. Well he tried it and when we saw him splashing thru we decided to find a better place to cross. We looked and found that it was the best place the river "afforded" and so I made a wild dash across. I went so quickly that I didn't get very wet. The other fellow had shorter legs than mine, so he splashed himself up to his hips. But the sun was so warm that it soon dried off. We then came back to town and got here just

about supper time. After supper we signed the payroll for June. Then I read my mail over again and then went down to the station and got a paper. Came back and went to bed. A most enjoyable day.

Juillet

"𝔅rite"& 𝔉air

Worked at the office all day. I found out to-day that they had me booked as a sort of draughtsman. That is, I will help out when I am not busy otherwise. I drew a set of drawing instruments. To-night we moved from our "mansion in the sky." We have two rooms over a garage in one of the swellest estates here in town. One of the rooms is finished off (I am in that one) and the other is a sort of storeroom (unfinished. To reach our quarters we have to ring a bell and the "concierge" presses a button and the gate opens. Then we go up a gravel walk with a big lawn on one side and a conservatory on the other, to the garage up in back. Up one flight and "voila" you are in our appartments. There are five of us in the room I am in and it is certainly a pleasant one. There are two windows in it one on the east and one on the south side. I think it will be a fine place for us.
No Mail to-day.

Juillet

"Brite & Fair" Nice day. [Crazy quilt (contours)]
Worked at the office all day. We were very busy so I worked until 9:00 P.M. Went down to the station to get a paper but they did not come on the train so went back to our appartment and went to bed.
Sent a postcard to Berta.
No Mail.

Juillet

Cloudy and rather cool all day.
Worked at the office all day. ~~Made some blue prints, in the~~
Wrote to Berta.
No Mail.
Paid to-day.

Juillet

Cloudy and cool all day. This is the Glorious 4th and a holiday over here. The
houses and stores all over town were decorated with the flags of the allied nations.
It was a very pretty sight to look up the main street and see all the different flags.
The "natives" were all out in their best Sunday go to meeting clothes. In one of
the squares there was a bandstand and we had a real American band play for us.
It certainly did sound fine. I had to work in the morning but had the afternoon
off. It was so cool that I did not go out, but went down to my billet and wrote
to A. Annie & U. Waldo. There were track events in the morning but as I was
working, I did not attend. In the afternoon there was a ball game. After supper
I did not go out but stayed in and read. When we came back from supper "P.K,"
sprung a good one. The kids over here never saw any chewing gum before, so
whenever you go out they are always asking you for some. Well "P.K." was
chewing some and a little girl came up and asked him for a piece of gum. "PK"
looked at her, took the piece out of his mouth and offered it to her. You should have
seen the face she made up. This noon I had a letter from Russell Leavitt.

Juillet

"Brite & Fair" Worked at the office all day. This noon we had "beaucoup" mail.
I had 10 letters from the following:- 3 from A. Annie & U. Waldo, 3 from Berta-
also 3 cards, 1 from Jim MacDonald, 1 from Bernice, 1 from "Al" Morse, and 1
from Jim Harrison. In one of A. Annie's & U. Waldo's were 3 pictures.
Made a sort of cabinet or rather a set of shelves for our "appartments." So each
fellow has a sort of shelf to keep his stuff on.
No Mail.

Juillet

6 SAMEDI Ste Lucie   187-178

"Brite and Fair"
Worked at the office all day.
Wrote to Walter & Dempsey.
No Mail.

Juillet

7 DIMANCHE St Elie   188-177

"Brite" & Fair.
Did not arise this morning until about 9 o'clock. Worked all day making blue prints. The work did not go very good. We worked all day and did not accomplish much. Rather discouraging.
No Mail.
Wrote to Ma.
We have electric lights in our billet. I went up town last night and got a bulb and socket. We got a piece of wire and hitched it up and now we have light. Went down to the station and got a paper. Came back to the billet and read my paper and then hit the hay.

Juillet

8 LUNDI Ste Virginie   189-176

Brite & Fair.
Worked all day making blue prints. The work did not go at all well to-day.
No Mail.
Went over to the station and got a paper. No news in it.

Juillet

9 MARDI St Cyrille   190-175

Rainy all day.
Worked at the office all day.
We are packing up and getting ready for our next move. There is a lot of conjecture about where we are going but no one really knows.
No Mail
Wrote to Berta (blue envelope) p.

Juillet

When I got up this morning it was raining but it cleared off and we had a very nice day.
We are all packed up and ready for our next move. This morning I worked all morning putting on a stencil on our boxes. As there was not much doing in the afternoon I came down to the billet and took a nap. After supper I wrote to A. Annie & U. Waldo and Jim Harrison. We had quite a thunder shower after supper. It rained "cats and dogs." Went over to the station and got a paper. Came back and hit the hay.
No Mail.

Juillet

"Brite and fair"
No work to do to-day. So I went over and took a bath. In the afternoon we drew our "iron kellys." In the afternoon there wasn't much doing so I wrote to Jim MacDonald. After supper we had to go up to the office and did a little work. No Mail.
Came back to the barracks and hit the hay.

Juillet

"Brite & Fair." Worked in the morning loading a truck and then three of us went around picking up officers baggage with a little push cart. We were all thru by noon. This noon we had some second class mail. I had three bundles of papers from U. Waldo and two copies of "Tufts Weekly."
This afternoon there was nothing to do so I came down to the billet and went to sleep.

Juillet

"Brite" & Fair. Got up early this morning and after breakfast we moved all our office stuff out on the sidewalk ready to be taken to the train by truck. After

this was done we did not have anything to do, so went down to the billet rolled my pack, packed my barracks bag and got ready for our departure. About 11:30 A.M. we had mess and then we took all our personal stuff over to the train. We rode in "style" having at our disposal 2 "side door pulmans." Instead of having an elaborate name on the side of our car like American pulmans, our cars were marked "Hommes 32 Chevaux 8." We had a flat wheel on our car and as we did not care for the aforesaid title we called it the "Sarah Bernhardt," but this name was not chosen on account of the flat wheel. Our supplies were packed in the two cars. The cars looked pretty full before we started but this was only "camoflage." After we got started we repacked it and (6) of us had half a car to ourselves. We had our bed ticks filled with straw and we put them on the floor. We also had seats so we were fixed up a good deal more comfortable than we would have been in 1st class compartments. About 2 P.M. the French trainman gave the signal, the engine gave a shrill shriek and we were off to somewhere else in France. The other 8 men were in the other car and were fixed up about the same as we were. This country thru which we passed. We left the hilly country and passed thru a rather flat one. About 7 P.M. we arrived at a station and made quite a stop there. There was a Red Cross relief station there and we went in and got a cup of hot coffee and a nice jam sandwich. Then we drew some rations. We got some canned roast beef and some of the new French hard tack. Now these French biscuits are very crisp; in fact you have to be careful not to drop one on your toe for fear of being eligible for a wound stripe. The best way to eat them is to let the train run over them in order to break them up. But care should be taken not to get too many on the track for fear of derailing the train. They last like an all-day "sucker" and are very effective as hand grenades at short ranges. After we had consumed some of the rations we sat out by the doors of "our car" and watched the scenery fly by. We had reading material to take up our spare time. At about 8:30 P.M. it started to rain, making it rather disagreeable sitting in the doorway, so most of us layed down on our bed ticks. It began to get dark so we started to turn in for the night. I staid up on guard until 11:30, and then I turned in. "Sarah" had a rather rough night with her one flat wheel. Her "shock absorbers" were also not in very good working order. After being tossed around for a while I finally got to sleep and managed to get a few hours sleep. Thus ended our first day touring France in a side door pulman.
No Mail.

This is the national holiday in France, commemorating the fall of the Bastille. I got up this morning about 5 o'clock and it was pretty cool. I got a sweater out of my barracks bag and then felt better. It was rather foggy and damp. We had some more of our "crisp" biscuits and roast beef for breakfast. One of the fellows brought out a can of peaches and they certainly did taste good. About 10 A.M. it started to rain and kept it up for some time. We were bound for a certain B. town, but the plans were changed and we came here. We arrived here about 2 P.M. By that time it had stopped raining. After the train stopped some trucks came down and we loaded our stuff on them. There was a little over 2 loads and we were waiting for the truck to return. While we were waiting an officer came up and told us to unload a car of gasoline. It was some job. We finally finished, loaded our truck, and came up to the building where we are to have our Headquarters. Then we had all the stuff to carry up-stairs. It was sure some job as some of the boxes were rather heavy. We cleaned the place out and had all the stuff put away by supper time. For a change in diet I decided to dine out this evening so another fellow and I started out to look for a place to eat. On our way we met another American soldier that was going for the same purpose. This fellow formerly belonged to the French Legion and had a "croix de guerre." When U. S. got into this scrap he was transferred into the A.E.F. He was a very interesting fellow and told us a lot about the front. We finally found a place and had a good feed. We had some kind of soup then beans with a pork chop and some salad. We brought our own bread. The fellow we picked up could talk French like a "native." He was in a French regiment and had to talk French all the time. After supper the other fellow and I left the restaurant and went in search of a bath house. We finally located one right on the river. We went down and, for 12 cents, had a nice warm shower bath. Came out from there and went back to H.Q. where we were to spend the night. I was pretty tired so I made up my bed and turned in. Before I got to sleep some one came in and said we were going to move again to-morrow. That means we will have to take all the stuff down stairs again. Not a very pleasant thought to go to sleep on. This town is right on a river and larger than the last one we were in. Built right over the river is a mill. Across the river just below the mill is a foot bridge from which you can see the 4 waterwheels turning. The river here is pretty wide and the fishing seems pretty good. Went up town and got a few post cards. On our way here we passed some double decker cars. To get to the upper compartment you go up on the outside on one end of the car.
No Mail.

Juillet

Cloudy. Got up this morning and rolled my pack. Went up and had breakfast. After that we moved all the stuff down stairs and out in front of the building. Then we waited for the trucks to come. Had dinner. About 3 P.M. they came around and said we would not leave to-day, so we moved all the stuff back inside. We were just getting settled for the night when the major came around and said to get the stuff ready as the trucks would be here to-night. We all got busy and in about 20 minutes we had all the stuff on the sidewalk again. Then we sat around waiting for the trucks. About 10 P.M. the major came around and said we might just as well go to bed as the trucks wouldn't show up until morning. We left a couple of fellows to guard the stuff. I was rather tired and disgusted with army efficiency in general so I went to bed. (Air raid.)
No Mail.

Juillet

This morning early someone came around and woke me up and told me it was raining out and we would have to carry in some of the supplies that might spoil. We will wear it all out handling it so many times. Went over to the French "Y" and had a cup of hot chocolate and some cookies. While I was over there I wrote to Berta. Came back to H.Q. and waited around for the trucks. They finally came and we loaded our stuff on. Had dinner and then started on our way. It was very hot but just as soon as we got started we didn't mind the heat. Rode all the rest of the day. Before I left I wrote to Berta.
There were quite a good display of fireworks to-night.
No Mail.
American & French offensive started on the Marne

Juillet

"Brite" & Fair.
We kept right on going and finally arrived at this place about 5 o'clock. We were pretty tired and lay right down under the trees and were soon sound asleep. It

rained while we were asleep but the trees acted as a fine shelter. We were up again and had breakfast. We certainly did look like a band of gypsies sitting around eating our breakfast. After we had had our breakfast we came up here. It is certainly a pretty place right in the woods. We are billeted in a house and another fellow and I have a room to ourselves. It is fixed up pretty nice. There are 2 homemade cots in the room and I have a feather bed on mine (pretty soft.) We also have two chairs and a table. It is a corner room and has two windows in it. Got kind of straightened around to-day.

No Mail

Added a little to Berta's letter.

Juillet

18 JEUDI St Camille   199-166

"Brite" & Fair

Nothing much to do to-day so I did a little washing. I got my clothes fairly clean. It was so nice and warm that they dried very quickly. I mended a pair of socks and made a darn good job of it. Then I puttered around all day doing little odd jobs.

We are certainly isolated here. It is just like camping out in the woods. If we stay here very long we will surely save money as there isn't even a chance to spend it. Had more fireworks to-day and to-night. Another fellow and I took a walk in the woods. We found a sort of rustic bench and it was certainly odd. The roof and sides in fact the whole thing was inlaid with twigs. There was also some writing put on in the same manner. "Cave."

No Mail.

Juillet

19 VENDREDI St Vincent de Paul   200-165

"Brite" & Fair.

In the morning we tried out some of our new gelatine and it worked fine. We also had a gas drill. The gas used was only a tear gas and not harmful. We took it in the basement of a little church in the woods. Then we came back and had dinner. After dinner we were detailed to go to a nearby town and help out with the wounded. We walked down and got there about 1 P.M. They were using a sort of castle as a hospital. It was hot out and the walk right after dinner kind of got me. I laid down for a few minutes and then felt better. We had not been there more than an hour when we were told to report back to our camp. We walked back and when we got there we found that we were off on another trip. We rolled

our packs and went by truck. It was some trip. When we got to our destination (Taillefontaine) we were divided into two groups and the group I was in was sent back to camp. We arrived here about 7 o'clock. We had supper then we were ordered to report to the hospital again. I was all in so did not go. But the other fellows did and worked all night. No Mail
A fine old castle "Pierrefonds"

Juillet

20 SAMEDI Ste Marguerite   201-164

Cloudy most all day
Nothing to do to-day but sleep and write letters. Wrote to Russell L., Bernice, "Al" Morse, and Ma.
No Mail
Heavy barrage all day.
To-night a bunch of Scotch kilties went by our place here. They were looking for a place to take a bath. At the end of the procession were two dressed in civilian clothes. One was dressed as a woman. He had on dresses and a hat and carried a sunshade. The other one was dressed as her husband and had on trousers, a black hat and carried a cane. They were walking arm in arm and they certainly did look funny.

Juillet

21 DIMANCHE St Victor   202-163

"Brite" & Fair
To-day being Sunday there was not much to do, so I wrote to A. Annie & Uncle Waldo. Then I read some. After supper P.K. and I took a walk. We saw a Scotch band all dressed up in their kilts.
No Mail.
We get our water from an old well and we have to pump it up by means of an old pump operated by a wheel and an eccentric. The water is very good. Nice and cool.
The buildings here are very pretty, all covered with ivy. The one opposite is just completely covered with only the windows showing.

Juillet

22 LUNDI Ste Madeleine   203-162

"Brite" & fair
There was not much doing so "P.K." and I took a transit out in the woods and tested it to see if it was adjusted right. It was in fine condition. We came back and by way of excitement I shaved off my mustache. When one of the fellows saw it I thought he would hurt himself laughing. I told him it was a good thing I didn't have a beard as the effect might be serious on him.
To-night we had mail. I had five letters. 2 from Berta, 1 from A. Annie & U, Waldo, 1 from Walter and 1 from K. Potter. It seemed good to hear from the folks again.

Juillet

23 MARDI St Appolinaire   204-161

Cloudy part of the day.
To-day we got our stuff packed up ready for our next move. It only took us about half a day. The rest of the day we just hung around and took life easy. This morning we had a little mail. I had a letter from Jim McHale and one from Beth dated June 25th with my new address on it. They certainly put a good one over on one of the fellows here. We are all looking for souvenirs; well one of the fellows found a piece of alluminum that came from an areoplane, in one of the rooms of our billet. He took it and gave it to a French interpreter and told him to give it to another fellow and tell him that it came from a German plane that bombed a nearby town. Well the fellow got it OK and has been around showing it to everyone and very proudly relating its "history." After supper "P.K." and I took a walk out in the woods.

Juillet

24 MERCREDI Ste Christine   205-160

"Brite & Fair"
We hung around all morning waiting for trucks to move our stuff. About noon one showed up and we loaded part of our stuff on it and sent it away right after dinner. We did not expect any more trucks but about 2 P.M. four more showed up. And we loaded the rest of our stuff on them and crawled up on top of the load. We had a couple of bed ticks full of straw so we fixed up a pretty comfortable seat on the back end of the truck. We got away about 4 P.M. and after about a 30 mile ride arrived at this place about 8 o'clock.

We got fixed up for the night. We are quartered over a stable that goes with a chateau; this chateau being better than the last one we were at. Like at the last place we are right in the middle of a forest. The nearest town is about a kilometre from here. There is a good sized lake here so we have a good chance to bath (it is not deep enough to swim in.) We sleep in wooden bunks (single) and they are pretty comfortable. The one I have is pretty wobbly but a few nails and a hammer will remedy the difficulty.
No Mail.

Juillet

25 JEUDI St Jacques maj.   206-159

"Brite & Fair
Worked all day up at the chateau getting our things fixed up. To-night after supper four of us took a walk to a town about 4 kilometers away, where there is a "Y." It was a very pleasant walk. On our way we heard a whip-o-will singing in the trees. We were able to get some chocolate and cookies at the "Y." It is a very pretty walk thru the woods and around by the lake.
No Mail

Juillet

26 VENDREDI Ste Anne   207-158

Brite & Fair most all day.
There was not much doing all day so I wrote some letters. I wrote to Berta, A. Annie & U. Waldo, Beth, Walter, Ma, and Katherine Porter. Now I am all caught up with my mail.
It clouded up right after supper. Another fellow and I decided to take a walk down to the "Y." We took our raincoats along and it was a good thing we did as the rain came down in torrents just as we were starting back. It did not last very long however. The sun came out and we had a double rainbow. One of them was very bright while the other one about thirty feet away was rather dim.
No Mail.

Juillet

27 SAMEDI Ste Nathalie   208-157

Brite & Fair
I was under the weather all day. My bowels had not been very regular so I took some pills yesterday. Consequently, I had a touch of disentary. I had a headache

all day and was certainly feeling mean. I ate a little breakfast and that was all I ate all day. I just laid around in my bunk all day.

We had beaucoup mail to-day. I had 5 letters from Berta (one having pictures in it); 5 from A. Annie & U. Waldo (one having pictures in it), and 1 from Lila. We had a heavy shower to-night.

Juillet

28 DIMANCHE St Nazaire   209-156

Cloudy most all day.

Felt better this morning. My headache was all gone but I had cramps in my stomach. I took things easy to-day and expect to be OK to-morrow.

No Mail.

Juillet

29 LUNDI Ste Marthe   210-155

"Brite & Fair"

Feeling much better to-day.

Worked to-day packing up our stuff ready for our next move. We were all thru by noon. This afternoon I laid around and read. No Mail.

Juillet

30 MARDI St Ignace d. L.   211-154

Got up in good season and after an early breakfast went up to the "chateau" to load a truck and get things straightened around. It was rather foggy but the sun came out and we had a nice day. We were all thru by noon. I felt much better to-day.

After dinner we went down to the lake. We had two boats and paddled all over the lake. Then we went ashore and caught some grass-hoppers and fished for a while but did not catch any fish. Then we decided to go for a swim. We found a nice deep place. I guess it was about 20 feet deep. We undressed on shore and went out in the boat in our "birthday clothes" We certainly had a nice swim. Came back to the billet and took it easy. No Mail

"Brite" & Fair.

This morning after breakfast we got all our stuff out and ready to go on the trucks. But the trucks didn't show up. We waited around and after an early dinner we loaded them up We got all our personal stuff together and climbed up on top of the load. When we were just comfortably settled five of us had to get off as there was too much load on. So we don't leave until to-morrow.

To-day I heard that I had been made a first class private. Just a rumor and I don't know if it is so or not.

No Mail

To-night I wrote to Lila

Août

"Brite" & Fair.
We had an early breakfast and then rolled our packs and were all ready for our next move. This time the "best" transportation we could get was a Dodge car. I sat in the front seat and it was certainly a fine trip. We had a little engine trouble so we stopped in a fairly large town for two hours. We had dinner there. After dinner we pushed on. Near the end of our journey we rode up a beautiful valley. It was pretty wide with the river in the middle. Some of the towns we passed thru were pretty well knocked to pieces. In the town where we are, there is not a whole roof. It is completely knocked to pieces. So we have plenty of ventilation. The room I sleep in has a hole about 8 feet in diameter, right in the wall. This place must have been a fine place in peace times, but now it is a wreck. We have a piano in one room that still has a few tunes in it. No Mail.

Août

Rainy all day.
This morning I worked around the office. As we finished up all the work there was not much doing in the afternoon. So I did some washing. I found a nice place in a nearby building where I could heat some water and boil my clothes. As I had a fire, some salt pork and plenty "pommes de terre," I made some French fried potatoes for myself. They were fine.
Wrote to Berta & Ma.
No Mail.

Août

Showery to-day.
Worked around the office on various jobs all day.
Had some more "French Fried" to-day.
Wrote to A. Annie & U. Waldo
No Mail.

Août

Showery to-day.
Worked all day around the office.
We got some grease at the kitchen and had "beaucoup" French Fried potatoes.
They were fine.
No Mail

Août

Cloudy and showery all day.
Got up early and packed up for our next move. The truck showed up about 9 o'clock (A.M.) and we loaded it up. As there was not enough room for all of us we had to wait until the truck came back. We did not expect it to-day so just made ready to spend another night here. Well after supper I had a nice fire going, had dug some potatoes, and had my mouth all set for some nice "French fried," when the truck showed up. I went right ahead and cooked one batch, and put them in my mess kit. Then we jumped on the truck. We did not get started until nearly dark. It was raining and the roads were pretty muddy. The towns thru which we passed were pretty well battered. It was pitch dark when we got here and we couldn't have a light. I slept down in a sort of cave.
We had mail to-day, all old. I had a letter from A. Annie & U. Waldo, one from Jim MacDonald, and a card signed by all the folks that were down home on July 4th.

Août

Cloudy and showery.
Got up this morning and had my "French fried" for breakfast. Then we all turned to and cleaned up the house here. It was a very different looking house when we got thru. I moved my bed from the cave, upstairs in the attic. This house seems to be in better condition than the last one we were at.
Worked around the office all day.
After supper went down to the "Y" and after standing in line for about an hour managed to get some smokes, chocolate, cookies, and a can of peaches. They all certainly tasted fine. I have enough tobacco to last me a month. Came back and worked until dark. No Mail.

Août

Cloudy most all day.
Worked at the office all day and came back after supper and worked until 10:30. We fixed the windows so that the light would not shine out.
There are sure a bunch of flies here. They are so tame you can't drive them away. Up around the mess tent (we eat in the open) they are just like bees around a hive. And the mud is between 3 and 6 inches deep and sticks to your feet just like glue. We have had so much rain that the roads are in pretty bad shape
No Mail.
Wrote to Jim MacDonald.

Août

Fair but cloudy in afternoon.
Worked in the office all day. We were pretty busy all day. In the afternoon "Fritz" got rather playfull and sent over some shells. You could hear them whistle as they went over and then you would hear the report when they struck. The first one made us sit up and take notice but after that we got used to them.
To-day we had mail. I had 2 bundles of papers from Uncle Waldo and a letter from A. Annie & U. Waldo and one from Ma.

Août

9 VENDREDI St Amour   221-144

"Brite" & Fair
Last night as a sort of precautionary measure, most of us slept in a cave downstairs. There were no rats so we slept pretty comfortably with the rumble of the big guns up on the front to lull us to sleep. Got up this morning in good season and worked all day in the office. We were pretty busy and the time passed pretty quickly. After supper we got an order from the "Lieut" and went down to the Y.M.C.A. storehouse and got a bunch of stuff. We got 4 dozen cans of peaches, some chocolate, some cookies, and some cigarettes. They were fine. No Mail. Not much excitement to-day.
Wrote to Berta.

Août

10 SAMEDI St Laurent   222-143

"Brite" & Fair
Busy all day at the office.
No Mail.
Wrote to A. Annie & U. Waldo.

Août

11 DIMANCHE Ste Suzanne   223-142

"Brite" & Fair
Worked all day. This noon we had mail. I had two letters & a card from Berta, a letter from Lila, and one from A. Annie & U. Waldo with two pictures in it.
The roads here are pretty well dried out so that there is not so much mud. According to the papers the British & French are making a big push up on the Albert front.

Août

12 LUNDI Ste Clair   224-141

Cloudy in the morning but it cleared up and we had a nice day. Worked in the office all day and was very busy. One of the fellows is sick so that makes so much more for the rest of us to do.
The church here in this town is in fairly good shape. To be sure the windows are all knocked out and there is a shell hole in one side. On the inside the altar is in

good condition, but all the pictures around the walls in the body of the church have been slashed out by the Germans when they made their rapid exit from here. No Mail.
Wrote to Ma.
Drew 2 suits of light underwear and 2 pair of socks to-day.
Signed the payroll for July.

Août

13 MARDI St Hippolyte   225-140

"Brite" & Fair.
Worked in the office all day. We were very busy and worked until about 10 o'clock. Then when we are all settled for a good night's sleep Fritz came over and dropped a few "calling cards." Three of them landed about 300 yards from here, which is close enough for comfort.
Had a couple of bunches of papers from U. Waldo. No first class mail.

Août

14 MERCREDI St Eusèbe   226-139

"Brite" & Fair.
Feeling kind of tired to-day as my sleep was somewhat disturbed last night.
Worked in the morning. We got things pretty well cleared up so I took a nap in the afternoon. Felt much better. To-night we had mail. It was all June mail. I had a letter from Phil Carr, one from Bernice and one from Berta. I also had 2 rolls of newspapers from Uncle Waldo.

Août

15 JEUDI Assomption   227-138

"Brite" & Fair
To-day we weren't very busy and I expected to have a chance to write a few letters but had just got started when they sent down from the other office for a man and I was elected. And they sure did keep me busy all day. I had to walk up and it was pretty warm. I worked until about 6 o'clock and then came back here. When I got back I found that we had had mail. I got 2 letters from A. Annie & U. Waldo and two from Berta. I took a shave and wrote a letter to Phil Carr.

Août

"Brite" & Fair
We were not very busy to-day so I got caught up on my mail. I wrote to Lila, Bernice, A. Annie & U. Waldo and Berta and Ma. It was some batch of letters and I am glad that I have them off my hands. I took a bath in a "cup" to-day and feel much better.
When I came from supper I saw a rather odd and at the same time funny sight. There were two white horses and evidently some one for a joke spotted them all over with black paint so that they were pretty well camoflaged.
Stopped at the "Y" and got a package of cookies.
No Mail.

Août

17 SAMEDI St Septime   229-136

"Brite" & Fair.
Worked at the office all day.
The people are gradually coming back to their homes here. This noon at dinner time there were quite a few natives down at the mess shack. They gave them something to eat, and took moving pictures of one old white haired woman, holding a mess kit in one hand and standing at the coffee can and getting a cup of coffee.
Sent the July 26th Stars and Stripes to Aunt Annie & Uncle Waldo.
No Mail

Août

18 DIMANCHE Ste Hélène   230-135

"Brite" & Fair
Busy in the office all day.
To-day we had mail. I had 2 letters from A. Annie & U. Waldo and 2 from Berta. About 7 P.M. the C.O. came round and told us to pack up as we were going to move to-morrow. So we got busy and were all packed up before dark.
Saw Q. Roosevelt's grave. It is all fenced in and on the grave are flowers and some of the parts of his machine. The epitaph says, "Died on the field of honor July 16th 1918.

After dark I took a picture of our dugout. We used some carbon lights and I took a time exposure.
We were shelled again to-night but none of the shells landed very close.

Août

19 LUNDI St Louis é.   231-134

"Brite" & Fair.
We got up in good season and were told to get some of the stuff outside ready to move before we went to breakfast. The result was, we lost our breakfast and I felt mean all day.
We had a nice ride by truck over pretty rough roads which shook our "breakfast???" down and arrived here about 11 A.M. We had dinner and felt a little better. Then we got our stuff straightened around. We were pretty well settled before supper time. On our way here we passed thru several towns and they were all pretty badly knocked to pieces. This town was the scene of some of the hardest of the fighting.
No Mail.
I was pretty tired and went to bed early.

Août

20 MARDI St Bernard   232-133

Cloudy in the morning, but fair and hot in the afternoon. I swept out this morning and then did a little drawing. Then I made some frames to cover up the windows at night so the light won't shine thru. I stopped work at 4 P.M. (being a union carpenter.) I washed up and then went out in the orchard back of our place. In "our" orchard we have apples and plums. The plums are just ripe and are nice and blue. One of the fellows said that if we ate too many of them we would get "Plumbego." The apples are not ripe yet
Had a Sunday Herald (July 21st) from U. Waldo.
Had a wonderful moon last night. It was nearly as bright as day. A wonderful night for an air raid but "Fritz" did not show up here.

Août

21 MERCREDI Ste Jeanne   233-132

"Brite" & Fair. Another hot day.
Worked part of the day in the office.
No Mail.
Full moon. Fritz came around and dropped a "card" but not in this neighborhood.

Août

22 JEUDI St Symphorien   234-131

"Brite" & Fair Another hot day.
There was not much doing so I wrote to Berta, & A. Annie & U. Waldo.
We had a very pretty sunset to-night. It was just as red as fire. Then the moon
came up and it was nice and bright.
No Mail.

Août

23 VENDREDI Ste Sidonie   235-130

"Brite" & Fair
Was under the weather all day. Had the dysentary I just laid around all day on
my bunk. At noon I had some mail. I had a letter from Berta, a card from "Art"
Waldron and 4 bundles of papers from U. Waldo.
After supper I went out and took a bath at our "wash stand." Felt good deal
cooler.
Had another pretty sunset to-night. This time it was a golden one.

Août

24 SAMEDI St Bartélemy   236-129

Cloudy all day.
Was not feeling any too good to-day so did not go to breakfast. We got paid this
morning. I drew 88 francs.
Took some laundry out to-day.
Felt better along to-wards night.
No Mail.

Août

25 DIMANCHE St Louis roi 237-128

"Brite" & Fair

Not much doing to-day. I mounted my map of France on "linen." Felt much better to-day. This noon I had a letter from Berta with 12 pictures of her Portland trip in it. They were very good. Also had a letter from Walter.

Wrote to Ma.

Août

26 LUNDJ St Zépherin 238-127

"Brite" & Fair. Feeling much better. Worked all day in the office. The people are coming back to this town by twos and threes. To-day the family that formerly lived here returned. They had what belongings they could carry packed on two two-wheeled carts. There was the man, his wife, and a whole raft of children. They also brought a cow along. We had to move our things out of their kitchen so they could have a place to cook. But we kept the rest of the house and I think they (the natives) sleep in the barn.

There are certainly a lot of shell holes around here. Some of them are about 15 feet in diameter and 10 feet deep.

The farmers here have cut their grain. They use an American binder and pile their bundles in piles that look much like our hay stacks. Then, since the barns are not water proof, they pile all the bundles in a big pile that are shaped some like a circus tent. The stacks are about 15 feet in diameter and about 20 feet high and are so piled that they shed water. I think the old mill in back of our domicile is where they thresh the grain. We had a shower in the night. No Mail.

Août

27 MARDI St Césaire 239-126

Cloudy in the morning but it cleared off about noon. I tried out a new mess-hall this last week and think we eat a little better there as there are not so many men eat there. The other morning we had flap-jacks and to-night we had ginger-bread. Very good. I got my laundry to-day and it only cost 3 francs. That is a good deal cheaper than I can do it and much easier. This noon I had a short letter from "Art" Waldron. Worked all day in the office. We had another shower during the night.

Darned my socks to-night.

Août

28 MERCREDI St Augustin   240-125

Cloudy.
This morning after I swept out, I went up and got a haircut. My hair was getting so long that I could nearly braid it. You see, I have not had a haircut for three months. It has been pretty chilly here the last few nights. When I came back from the barber shop I stopped at the supply room and drew a new pair of trousers. This noon I had a letter from A. Annie & U. Waldo.
Had another shower to-night

Août

29 JEUDI Déc. St J. - B.   241-124

Cloudy.
Worked in the office all day.
Wrote to "Art" Waldron.
No Mail.

Août

30 VENDREDI St Fiacre   242-123

Fair in the morning but cloudy in the afternoon
We were very busy to-day and had to work to-night until 10 P.M. There is a new commissary opened up about 2 kilometers from here. They are pretty well stocked up now but expect that the stock won't last long as we have not been near a "Y" or commissary for nearly two months
Wrote to A. Annie & U. Waldo.
No Mail
Had flap-jacks for breakfast & cookies for supper.

Août

Cloudy most all day
We were pretty busy all day.
This morning we had cookies for breakfast.
Wrote to Berta to-night
   "   " Ma   " "
   "   " Walter " "
No Mail.

Septembre

Cloudy all day.
To-day I got back on my Dorel job. Ever since we joined the corps it has not been working right. Well the "Lieut" went to Paris and got some new gelatine and ink and I think it is going to work now. We tried some to-day and they seem O.K. This noon we had mail. I had a letter from A. Annie & U. Waldo, one from "Shep" and one from Berta with some pictures in it. I also had two bundles of papers (June 22nd, June 23rd) from U. Waldo.
I was pretty tired and went to bed early. It came pretty cool along to-ward morning but I had plenty of blankets so I slept warm.

Septembre

"Brite" & Fair all day. This being Labor Day we did a big days work. The Dorel process was working good. It is some consolation to work on a job and get results. The way it was before we would work all day and not get a single good copy. This was very discourageing. But I think we are coming O.K. now. This morning we had flapjacks for Breakfast and they were fine. Then one of the fellows had a little spare time and went over to the commissary and got quite a little stuff. Out of the lot I split a can of lemon drops and a can of stick candy with another fellow and had a whole can of grape juice jam. It was fine. We worked until about 10 P.M. and then I had some bread and jam. Pretty cool again to-night. No Mail. Signed the payroll for August.

Septembre

3 MARDI St Grégoire   246-119

Cloudy in the morning but fair in the afternoon. Worked all day on the Dorel process and had very good luck. We worked until about 8 P.M.
Over at H.Q. the men sleep on the second floor and in order to get to their quarters they have to use a ladder. One of the fellows picked up a little fox terrier somewhere and the dog goes up and down the ladder just as nice as can be.
No Mail.

Septembre

4 MERCREDI Ste Rosalie   247-118

We had flap-jacks for breakfast. It was pretty cool when we get up in the morning. Worked all day on the Dorel process.
No Mail.
We had a thunder shower about 6 P.M.

Septembre

5 JEUDI St Bertin   248-117

When we got up this morning it was raining but it cleared off about 10 A.M. and we had a nice day.
Was not doing much this morning so I wrote some letters.
Wrote to H.N. Shepherd (24 Gilbert Street, Lynn, Mass.)
     "   "   Berta
     "   "   A. Annie & U. Waldo
     "   "   Ma.
No Mail.

Septembre

6 VENDREDI St Onésiphore   249-116

"Brite" & Fair
Not much to do to-day, so just took life easy. Darned a pair of socks.
Last night a couple of the fellows thought of a new game. They found 4 old bayonets and drew the outline of Kaiser Bill on a board and then would stand off about 10 feet and throw the bayonets at "Bill." If you hit him in the body it counted one, in the head two, and if you hit him in the eye you got 5. They set the

mark at 50 and the one that reached that number first was the winner.
No Mail.

Septembre

7 SAMEDI St Cloud   250-115

"Brite" & Fair. Did one job on the Dorel and got fine results.
Then as there was no more work to do I made two dozen envelopes.
For supper we had a sort of prune pie and it was fine. No Mail.

Septembre

8 DIMANCHE La Nativite   251-114

Cloudy & Rainy all day
To-day we packed up our stuff and in a short time we were ready for our next
move. As there was not much to do another fellow and I went to the commissary.
We got some jam (raspberry), stick candy, lemon drops, cigarettes, and canned
frankforters. It was quite a walk and the road was pretty muddy. However we
reached our destination without any mishap and got our stuff. It was quite a load
but we caught a truck on the way back.
After supper four of us went up to the kitchen to draw some rations We got
46lbs. of canned meat and 60lbs. of hard tack. It was packed in two boxes. They
gave us a two wheeled truck like they use to truck freight. The roads were very
rough and muddy. We wired the 2 boxes to our truck and started for our billet.
I was on the handles and it was just like plowing rough, rocky ground. It was a
good thing it was all downhill but at that it was pretty rocky sailing.
Then some of us went up to the lithograph shop and played cards until about 10
o'clock. We had the windows all camoflaged and the roof was tight, and a nice
fire in the fireplace. After the card game was over we had a little lunch. I opened
up a can of frankforts and another fellow opened up some jam. We all had bread
that we brought from the kitchen. We roasted the "weenies" over the fire and they
were fine. While I was roasting one of my "dogs" he fell on the floor but I gave
him a bath and a rub down with a piece of paper and he was in fine condition.
We had toast and jam also. After our feed I came back to the billet and the "dogs"
growled all night.
Had a letter from Berta.

Septembre

Fair in the morning.
We got all packed up and then waited for the trucks. When I came back from breakfast I stopped to get a canteen of water. The place where we get our water is at a sort of wash house. It looks some like a swimming pool with stone sides that slope down to the water. When I stopped there there was a woman doing her washing and with her was her little daughter. I don't think the little girl was more than five years old and she was down on her knees scrubbing like a good one.

About noon the trucks came and we loaded them up and then we climbed up on top and left about 2 P.M. It was a very pretty ride right down a valley. We passed thru several towns and they all looked as though a hurricane had blown off the roofs. After about a 12 mile ride we came to the R.R. where we stopped and unloaded our trucks. It started to rain so we had to cover up the goods. After waiting a while a freight train pulled in and we loaded our stuff onto a flat car and covered it with tarpaulin. Then we went to our box car where we were to ride. We had our bed sacks with us and spread them out on the floor of the car. About 9 P.M. we pulled out. It was very cloudy. I brought along some bread, butter and "weenies" for lunch and they certainly tasted fine. As there was nothing to see we went to bed and slept pretty well.
No Mail.

Septembre

Rainy & Pretty cold.
When we woke up it was raining. Our car leaked and we got a little damp. We finally arrived at our destination at about 9:45 A.M. and the rain was coming down in sheets. We stayed on the side track until about 1 o'clock hoping that the rain would stop but no such luck. Some trucks came down and we loaded part of the stuff onto them. The rest we unloaded from the car and covered it with canvas. Then we waited around for the trucks to come back. It was pretty cold and we were pretty wet. Finally a truck came and we loaded the rest of the stuff on and as I was kind of cold I decided to walk to town which was only about 1$^1/_2$ miles. The roads were pretty muddy but we didn't mind that. By the time I reached the town I was nice and warm. I got my barracks bag and changed my clothes and felt better. Then we opened some hash and had some hard tack with it.

Then we were assigned to our billet. It is in a room that was roughly boarded up in a stable. However we are pretty comfortable as we have bunks and electric lights. There is a dirt floor. We slept very comfortable to-night.

This town is quite a place. It has not been held by the Germans and is in good condition. There are several deep dugouts here.
No Mail.

Septembre

11 MERCREDI St Hyacinthe   254-111

Rain.
Got up this morning and found it was still raining. Went to breakfast. Then brought our barracks bags up to our billet. There was not much work to do so I did some writing. We played cards and dominoes and took life easy. Wrote a blue letter to Berta and a letter to A. Annie & U. Waldo.
No Mail.

Septembre

12 JEUDI St Raphaël   255-110

Cloudy when we got up this morning. Reported at the office after breakfast but as there was no work to do, I came back to the billet. Reported back to the office after dinner and was assigned as barracks orderly for the afternoon. Wrote a letter to Ma then I repacked my barracks bag.

In our billet we have company. This time it is mice. It was funny the other night. I woke up and heard a funny noise over in the corner. I listened and heard this fellow saying "sh, sh," as if he was trying to scare something away. This evidently didn't work as pretty soon I heard him trying to imitate a cat by running his fingers up and down the blankets. I guess it worked as I didn't hear any more. No Mail.

Septembre

13 VENDREDI St Maurille   256-109

"Brite" & Fair "Friday the 13th"
To-day an order came out that the enlisted men would have to turn in their barracks bags. The "non-coms" were allowed to keep theirs. So we picked over our stuff, kept what was necessary, threw away, gave away or turned in what we didn't need. You would be surprised how hard it was to give things away; it was nearly impossible to give your things away. I did manage to give away a helmet

and some handkerchiefs. However I saved all my winter wear. We got paid for August this noon. I drew 188 francs.

In the afternoon I worked at the office. Then just before supper I turned in my barracks bag. I kind of hated to see it go. But after supper I made a small box large enough to take what I had left.

I had to work a little while after supper finishing packing up. Then I came back and packed my box.

No Mail.

Had a bundle of papers from U. Waldo (July 26th)

Septembre

14 SAMEDI Ex. Ste Croix   257-108

"Brite" & Fair. Got up this morning about 5:30 and went down to breakfast. We had to be down there by 6:00 if we wanted to eat. I made it O.K, but some of the fellows were out of luck. We rolled our packs and tied on what extra stuff we had. I put my box on the truck with the rest of the office supplies. We loaded up our stuff in a hurry and were ready to leave by 8:00 A.M. We did not make a very long jump this time. We reached here about 9:30 A.M. and unloaded our stuff. This time our office is in a wooden barracks that has been partitioned off and a floor put in. I have been put in charge of the "Dorel Process" according to the dope now.

We sleep in a wooden barracks not far from the office. We have "double decker" bunks and I have a "lower berth" I think we should be very comfortable here. This is only a small town and there are not many "natives" here

No Mail.

Just before I went to bed another fellow and I took a walk. It was rather cloudy but the temperature was just right for a walk. Came back to the barracks and slept fine.

Septembre

15 DIMANCHE St Nicomède   258-107

"Brite" & Fair. A fine day. Did some work on the Dorel to-day and had pretty good results in the morning but it came off hot in the afternoon and the gelatine got so sticky we had to stop work. Then I went to work on another job. Worked awhile after supper.

We had a nice moon light night to-night. No Mail.

Septembre

"Brite" & Fair. Another nice warm day. Did not work on the Dorel to-day but had several other small jobs to-day. Came back from supper and worked awhile. Then I went up to the orchard and got some apples. They were not quite ripe but they tasted pretty good.

This afternoon I had a card that was signed by all the folks that were at Conway on August 9th.

This has been a very warm day and I hope we have lots more of them.

We have a sales commissary just across the street from our office. To-night I had to work. Had an air raid.

Septembre

Rainy & Cloudy in the morning but Fair in the afternoon

Finished the job I was working on at 3 A.M. As I was pretty tired and didn't want to get up for breakfast this morning, I had a lunch before turning in. Opened up a can of salmon and had that with bread. Got to bed about 3:30 and did not get up until about 10. Came over to the office and one of the fellows had some bread and jam that he said I could have. Built a fire in the little shack in back of the office, toasted the bread and made a cup of bullion. So I had quite a breakfast. By the time I had finished it was time to eat dinner. Did not work this afternoon. Just hung around the barracks.

Had a letter from Jim Harrison

Wrote to Berta & A. Annie & U. Waldo.

Septembre

Cloudy & Rain

We were not very busy to-day so I wrote to Ma in the morning and to Jim Harrison. In the afternoon I did a little work. We have a sort of club house where we can read, write, and play cards. It is a small barracks partitioned off into two rooms. In the front room there is a big fireplace and a table and some benches. In the other room there is a big table with benches around it. It is nice and comfortable in there. No Mail.

Septembre

Cloudy & Rainy all day
Worked in the morning on the cyclostyle and in the afternoon went to the Dorel.
The weather was pretty poor and I did not get very good results. This afternoon
we had mail. I had letters from Berta, Ma, A. Annie & U. Waldo, Jim, and Mary.
It was all old mail dated the last of July and the first of August.
This morning one of the fellows bought a five pound can of butter and five of us
split it up. It cost 54 cents a pound.
To-day some Frenchmen moved into our club house so we lose that.

Septembre

Cloudy and Rainy all day, Worked on the Dorel but did not get any results. It
was rather damp and chilly all day.
No Mail
This French mud over here is certainly treacherous stuff to walk on. It is slipperier
than ice and stickier than glue.
The chow here is not up to par. It being difficult to get rations.

Septembre

Cloudy & Rainy
For breakfast this morning we had rice, "monkey meat" and biscuits (2). We had
to wait for the biscuits, but they were worth it.
Nothing doing in the office this morning so I went over to the commissary and
got some strawberry preserves, and some milk. Then as it was damp and chilly
we built a fire in the shack in back of the office.
Not much doing in the afternoon, so I took a nap.
No Mail.

Septembre

Cloudy & Rainy all day.
Made some blue prints to-day. It was a pretty poor day but I got some pretty good results. All day long we had local showers and it certainly did rain hard.
Still no mail. I can't understand it. We have had no mail dated later than August 10th.
Played cards (casino) awhile and then went to bed and read awhile. I am reading "Contrary Mary."

Septembre

Cloudy & Rainy all day.
There was not much doing to-day so I took it easy. To-night I have to work. It might be an all night job.
To-day is the first day of fall and it was pretty damp and chilly. We had a fire in the shack in back of our office to-day and that took the chill off.
Went over to the commissary this morning but they had sold everything eatable so I came away empty handed.
Still no mail. My last letter from home is more than a month and a half old. When we do get mail we should have a raft of it.
We can buy milk in this town. It cost about 8 cents for a canteen full.
Worked until 12 o'clock to-night. Then I made some bullion and had some bread and butter before going to bed.

Septembre

"Brite" & Fair.
Did not get up until about 10 o'clock and then I came down to the office and made some toast and had that with a canteen of milk for breakfast. It tasted fine. Then I went to work cutting paper and while I was working I cut my finger and thumb.
This noon when we went up to dinner we had to get meal tickets. It seems that we have been feeding more men than we draw rations for. So to-day they thought they would "get a line on" the number of men they are feeding. This is one reason

we have not been eating any better. Now to-night we had beef steak, mashed potatoes, bread, coffee & cake, the best meal we have had for some time.
Had a letter to-day from Wesley MacSorley.

Septembre

25 MERCREDI St Firmin   268-97

Fair most all day. We had a shower in the afternoon.
To-day I worked all day draughting. This is the first time I have done any drawing for over a year. Felt a little awkward at first but after a little practice I think I will get my hand in again.
No Mail.
Wrote to Berta.

Septembre

26 JEUDI Ste Justine   269-96

"Brite" & Fair
Worked this morning draughting. It was pretty cold working this morning and we had to stop every once in a while to rub our hands to get them warm. This afternoon I went over to the commissary and bought a five pound can of butter (15.50f) Four of us divided it.
Wrote to Ma & A. Annie & U. Waldo.
No Mail.

Septembre

27 VENDREDI St Cosme   270-95

"Brite" & Fair.
Last night I was asleep and dreaming that I met "Bob" Parker over here when I heard an explosion or rather four of them. I woke up and some of the fellows were making for a dugout near our barracks. "Fritz" had come over and dropped a few bombs about a half mile away. The fellows getting out made more noise than the bombs did. It was the case of locking the barn after the horse has been stolen. This noon we had mail. I had a letter from Beth with some pictures in it, 2 letters from Berta, one of them had a nice silk handkerchief in it. And 3 letters from A. Annie & U. Waldo. One of the letters had a menu of the Adams House at Marblehead. I tacked the menu up on the wall and we look it over and decide what we will have for supper. One of the fellows was looking it over and said

"It's pretty near the end of the month, where is something for fifteen cents. We are not very busy right now.

Septembre

28 SAMEDI St Exupère   271-94

Fair in the morning but cloudy and cool in the afternoon. We were not busy to-day. That is the way our work goes. We will be rushed with work for a while then we will not have a thing to do.
We have the cutest little kitten you ever saw. He is a tiger and as one of the fellows remarked, he sounds just like a "boche" plane when he starts to purr. We feed him on milk and once in a while he catches a mouse.
Every day I get a canteen full of milk and it goes fine with buttered toast.
To-night we built a fire in the shack in back of the office and made some fudge. It burnt on a little but that gave it a flavor. We did not throw it away.
Wrote to Jim & Mary. Then I pasted some of my pictures in back of this book. No Mail.

Septembre

29 DIMANCHE St Michel   272-93

Rainy & disagreeable all day.
Worked this morning draughting
At noon we had mail. I was very fortunate and received 8 letters:- 2 from Walter, 1 from Ma, 1 from Beth, a birthday card from Berta, and three letters from U. Waldo & A. Annie. In one of the letters was a letter from Ruth.
Nothing in the afternoon so we built a fire out in the shack and tried to keep warm. After supper I wrote a little and read the paper.

Septembre

30 LUNDI St Jérôme   273-92

Cold and windy all day.
Nothing doing all day so we just hung around and tried to keep warm. We had a fire in our little shack but the wind was just right to make it smoke "fine."
After dinner went down street and got some hazelnuts. They were fine. This afternoon my old bunkie (the one I slept with last winter) called and we had quite a chat. Wrote to Wesley MacSorley.   No Mail.

"The Cootie"

A very affectionate little beast that sticks to you like an old friend or a plugged nickel. At times very playfull and will nip you in a very playfull manner and is very active especially at night when he comes out to exercise. As a report would read, he is very active on the "American front." There are various methods used to rid oneself of this uninvited guest. The most effective way is as follows:- Soak your clothes in a very strong solution of "NaCl" (commonly called salt) and take your clothes out and put them to dry near a river. When the cooties go to get a drink at the river grab the clothes and run like --- Sam Hill. The cooties will return find their home gone and nine times out of ten die of starvation and the other tenth will die of loneliness. "Fini cooties."

Octobre

1 MARDI St Rémi   274-91

Cloudy & Pretty cool. The work has fallen off so there is hardly a thing to do. Just took things easy and rested up. We had a fire in the shack in back of the office and we spent most of our time there. To-day I thought I had the French itch again but on close examination discovered I had acquired the "cooties." I captured two of them and ended their careers on the spot.
To-night we went down street and got some more nuts. They were fine. I was saying to-night that I guessed I had a cold in my head. One of the fellows spoke up and said, 'There is plenty of room there." How's that for a slam.
No Mail.

Octobre

2 MERCREDI Ste Anges gardiens   275-90

"Brite" & Fair. Not so cold as yesterday. To-day we were not very busy. I did one little job in the morning. Captured a few more cooties to-day.
This noon I had four bundles of papers from U. Waldo.
To-day we got our "club room" back. If we stay here very long the big fireplace will come in handy. Had to work until about 10 o'clock to-night. To-day our little kitten "done gone" died. Think he ate something that poisened him.

Octobre

3 JEUDI St Faust   276-89

Cloudy but not very cool.
Did a little carpentering this morning (putting a latch on a door.) Went on a still hunt to-day and bagged six cooties. This is the best I have done for some time.

This noon I had a letter from Lila (Aug 21st). In the garden in back of our office there are lots of sugar beets and other vegetables.

Worked on a job in the afternoon and after supper went over to the "club house" and wrote some letters. We had a fire in the fireplace. Wrote to Ma.

Went back to the office about 11 P.M. and had to go to work on a rush job. Worked nearly all night.

Octobre

4 VENDREDI St François d'Ass.   277-88

Cloudy and pretty cool this morning. Finished up my job about 3:30 this morning. Got to bed about 4 A.M. Just as I was getting to sleep they put up a heavy barrage up front. There sure is something doing up there to-day. Got up this morning for breakfast then went back to bed and stayed there until dinner time. Got up for dinner and then came over to the club house and built a fire in the fireplace. Then I wrote to A. Annie & U. Waldo. Had a letter from Berta and a card from Gertrude Ela.

Went to supper and came back and wrote to Walter.

A funny incident happened last night when we returned to barracks. There has been another outfit bunking with us for a few days. They pulled out last night and when we returned two of the fellows discovered that some of their stuff was missing. One fellow lost his toilet kit and the other one lost some books and some papers. They left a bible for the fellow who lost his papers signifying "the Lord be with you." The other one found a song book that meant he could whistle for his toilet kit. We laughed and joked about it. This is the first time any of us have missed anything since we have been in the army

Octobre

5 SAMEDI St Placide   278-87

Rather foggy in the morning but it cleared off and we had a pretty good day altho it was rather chilly. Worked in the morning doing a little drawing. In the afternoon two of us set up a couple stoves. Getting stoves looks as if we are going to be here for some time, but you can never tell. This after-noon I had a letter from Berta. To-night they set the clocks back an hour so we will have an extra hours sleep. This will make up for the hour we lost last March. Wrote to Berta. Got a can of jam and some to-bacco to-day. Had a nice fire in the fireplace in the "club room." It was nice and warm.

Octobre

Cloudy and cool all day. This morning put up some camoflage over one of the windows. Then some of us went on a wood detail to get fire wood. Came back and shaved. We are not very busy. This morning we had more mail. I had 2 letters and a card from Berta, a letter from Ma, one from A. Annie & U. Waldo, and one from "Art" Waldron.
Wrote to Lila
Caught 7 more cooties to-night.
In one of Berta's letters there was a picture of some men in the Topographical Section drawing maps in back of the front. The officer in the picture is our "Lieut." So I gave him the picture.
To-day we had a service in back of our office. There was an American band here and it certainly sounded fine

Octobre

Cloudy all day
Nothing doing to-day so I put the battle line up to October 1st on my map. Got some cheese down street to-day and it was fine. We had a fire in the fireplace in the club house and we played cards & read and wrote some. About supper time it started to rain and rained nearly all night. Signed the September payroll to-night.
Wrote to "Art" Waldron.
No Mail.

Octobre

Rainy and disagreeable all day. Nothing doing this morning so I made some envelopes. After dinner I went up to our little "two by four" bath house and had a nice warm shower bath. The water is heated in a small tank up over a small heater which burns wood. The water has to be pumped into the tank by hand. There are six showers and there is water enough comes thru to get a fair bath. Came back to the "club rooms" and played cards awhile. Had two letters from A. Annie & U. Waldo.

Octobre

9 MERCREDI St Denis évêque   282-83

"Brite" & Fair
*Not much doing to-day. So we took things easy. In the afternoon two of us put
up some camoflage around the office. To-night just about supper time we saw a
wonderful sight. A bunch of American planes flew over to-ward the front line.
They looked like a flock of birds. One of the fellows counted 87 planes that you
could see at one time.*
This noon we had mail. I had a letter from Ma, one from Lila & one from Berta.

Octobre

10 JEUDI St Paulin   283-82

"Brite" & Fair
*To-day I worked on the "Dorel process. I had quite a little trouble with it at first
and experimented with it during the morning. I finally found the trouble was the
blue print paper. In the afternoon I got some pretty fair results. No Mail.
To-night about 8 o'clock we had an air raid. "Fritz" came over and dropped a
few. None of them hit very near but they were close enough to shake the building.*

Octobre

11 VENDREDI Ste Clémence   284-81

*Cloudy all day. It was too cloudy to do much on the "Dorel," so took things easy
and wrote some. Wrote to Berta & A. Annie & U. Waldo. After supper I worked
until about 9 o'clock and then went to bed. My feet were wet from this mud we
have over here and I was feeling kind of mean. No Mail.*

Octobre

12 SAMEDI St Séraphin Columbus Day   285-80

*Cloudy and damp all day. I was under the weather with a sore throat. I got up for
dinner but went back to bed again. I was feeling pretty mean.
No Mail.*

Octobre

13 DIMANCHE St Edouard   286-79

Rainy & Drizzly all day. Last night I had a high fever. I decided to sweat my cold out so piled all my clothes on the bunk. I certainly did sweat. Felt a little better this morning. Got up for my meals but went right back to bed again. Had 4 bundles of papers from U. Waldo.

Octobre

14 LUNDI St Calixte   287-78

Cloudy & Disagreeable all day. Got up in the morning and came down to the office but was feeling pretty "rocky." Went down street and got some grapes. Hung around for a while and then went back to bed. Got up and had a little supper, took a physic and went to bed.

Octobre

15 MARDI Ste Thérèse   288-77

Another nasty damp disagreeable day. Did not get up until about supper time. Had 3 letters from A. Annie & U. Waldo and one from Walter. Felt much better to-night. Came down to the office and shaved and got cleaned up. Went up street and got a canteen of milk. It tasted pretty good. To-night it is raining again.

This is the final entry recorded by my Grandfather in his diary. He and the diary returned Stateside in August 1919 unharmed.

Bonnin, rue d'Anjou, 20.   Fagniez, r. d'Am   Norgeot, rue Tiquetonne, 64.
Boudin, rue Baillif, 5.   Ferté, r. des Pet.-Champs, 36.

U.S. TRANSPORTS IN A COLLISION; DODGE TORPEDO

Boston Record.
Nov. 23, 1917

Vessels on Way to France Report a Voyage Full Of Thrills

A FRENCH PORT—The latest American transports to reach here had an exciting trip through the submarine zone.

The first night in the zone two transports were in collision. One was slightly damaged while the other had a small hole torn in her bow and a few projecting guns damaged. Temporary repairs were made and the ships proceeded.

The following night a submarine attacked the transports. The wake of a torpedo was seen off the bow of one of the vessels, but no conning tower or periscope was visible.

The transports raced ahead and succeeded in reaching port safely, where the collision damage was repaired.

Boston Record,
November 23rd 1917

NOTES

P.K. Bunn
La Cross, Kansas

Fred A. Fenton
Stetson Hotel
907 Boren Ave.
Seattle, Washington

Roy L. Sacksteder
723 S. Ludlow St.
Dayton, Ohio

Lester N. Pressley
Ithaca, Michigan

Wesley B. Meyers
364 Oak Place
New Haven, Conn.

George N. Parkman
10 Willow St.
Holyoke, Mass.

NOTES

Thomas C. Miller
Penn B'l'dg'.
Erie, Penn.

Sigfred G. Christensen
112 Winnipeg Ave.
St. Paul, Minn.

David R. Evans
Nanty Glo, Pa.

Felix Formica
305 East 31st St.
New York City

Oscar F. Lohmann
2406 Hanover Ave.
Richmond, Va.

Henry D. Holtz
Harrisburg, Pa. (Susquehanna) 1225

NOTES

Left	Camp Devens U.S.A.	Oct. 28, 1917 - 4P.M.
Arrived	Hoboken	Oct. 29, 1917 - 10 A.M.
Left	Hoboken	Oct. 31, 1917 - 4P.M.
Arrived	Brest, France	Nov. 12, 1917 - 7A.M.
Left	Brest, France	Nov. 17, 1917 - 10A.M.
Arrived	St Nazier	Nov. 18, 1917 - 4A.M.
Left	St Nazier	Dec. 1, 1917 - 4P.M.
Arrived	Langres	Dec. 3, 1917 - 5P.M.
Left	Langres	June 1, 1918 - 8A.M.
Arrived	Mussy Sur Seine	June 1, 1918 - 2:30P.M.
Left	Mussy Sur Seine	June 14, 1918 - 7 A.M.
Arrived	Remiremont	June 15, 1918 - 2:30A.M.
Left	Remiremont	July 13, 1918 - 1:30P.M.
Arrived	Meaux	July 14, 1918 - 2:00P.M.
Left	Meaux	July 16, 1918 - 1:30P.M.
Arrived	Chateau Pierre Fonds La Chenoye	July17, 1918 - 5:00A.M.
Left	Chateau La Chenoye	July 24, 1918 - 4:00P.M.
Arrived	Le Chateau Mort Fontaine De Vallière	July 24, 1918 - 8:30P.M.
Left	Le Chateau De Vallière	August 1, 1918 - 9:00A.M.
Arrived	Gland	August 1, 1918 - 4:00P.M.
Left	Gland	August 5, 1918 - 7:30P.M.
	Captured by Americans Aug 2nd. 1918	
Arrived	Coulounge	August 5, 1918 - 10:30P.M.
Left	Coulounge	August 19, 1918 - 9:30A.M.
Arrived	Fresnes	August 19, 1918 - 11:00A.M.
Left	Fresnes	September 9, 1918 - 2:00P.M.
Arrived	Souilly	September 10, 1918 - 9:30A.M.
Left	Souilly	September 14, 1918 - 8.00A.M.
Arrived	Rampont	September 14, 1918 - 10:00A.M.

Appendix

Genealogy of the Ela Family

DANIEL ELA
There is no definitive proof that this is the first Ela in the American family tree.
b. ? 1631 d. 22 December 1710
wife: Elizabeth
two sons

ISRAEL ELA
b. 1655 d. 29 March 1700
wife: Abigail Bosworth
three sons, two daughters

SAMUEL ELA
b. 17 January 1684 d. 23 April 1742
wife: Hannah Clark
four sons, five daughters

ISRAEL ELA
b. 9 October 1711 d. 12 May 1753
wife: Terzah Ordway
five sons, two daughters

ISRAEL ELA
b. 12 April 1748 d. 23 May 1825
wife: Betsey Colby
five sons, one daughter

JONATHAN ELA
b. 24 June 1773 d. 3 May 1828
wife: Jerusha Martin
two sons, four daughters

SETH ELA
b. 31 March 1801 d.?1870
wife: Caroline Clark
two sons

CHARLES CLARK ELA
b. 27 December 1834 d. 29 August 1868
wife: Abby Melissa Perkins
one son, one daughter

CHARLES FRED ELA
b. 7 March 1862 d. 23 March 1936
wife: Mary Belle Blazo
two sons, three daughters

ROBERT BLAZO ELA
b. 17 September 1891 d. 1 October 1960
wife: Mary Alberta Martin
three sons, one daughter

Genealogy of the Blazo Family

WILLIAM BLAZO
Emigrated from Gironde, Aquitane, France and settled in New Hampshire
b. 1690? d. 14 August 1761
wife: Katherine Berry
large family

AMOS BLAZO
b. 3 December 1738 d. 23 February 1821
wife: Joanna Libby
six sons, three daughters

DANIEL BLAZO
b. September 1754 d. 19 January 1802
wife: Abigail Chapman
three or four children

ROBERT TIBBETS BLAZO
b. 11 August 1797 d. 24 May 1890
wife: Mary "Polly" Freeman
four children

DANIEL OTIS BLAZO
b. 6 November 1836 d. 22 August 1914
wife: Emily Perkins
one son, three daughters

MARY BELLE BLAZO
b. 3 February 1865 d. 21 June 1934
husband: Charles Fred Ela
two sons, three daughters

ROBERT BLAZO ELA
b. 17 September 1891 d. 1 October 1960
wife: Mary Alberta Martin
three sons, one daughter

Daniel O. Blazo

Emily (Perkins) Blazo
Mrs Daniel O. Blazo

The Blazo Grandparents

Mary (Blazo) Ela - daughter of Daniel & Emily

Pa's Mother

The Blazo-Leavitt House
(Taken from the internet - Wikipedia)

The Blazo - Leavitt House is a large two-story white-clapboard mansion built in Parsonsfield, Maine, in 1812 by William Blazo, uncle to prominent Parsonsfield lawyer Robert Tibbetts Blazo. Oral tradition holds that Robert T. Blazo, as a young man of fifteen in 1812 and later aged twenty in 1817, had helped with the construction of his uncle's house. This story seems credible because Robert had been bound out to his uncle William when Robert's father (William's brother) Daniel Blazo fell from a beam at a barn raising in 1802 and broke his neck. Later, ownership of the house passed to the nephew, Robert T. Blazo. The house next was passed on to Robert Blazo's two daughters, Susan Blazo Leavitt and Emily Blazo Browne. Emily's daughter Maude Browne left no descendants, and the house eventually passed into the hands of Susan Blazo Leavitt's son, Robert Greenleaf Leavitt, his wife Ida Ruggli Leavitt and his three children Russell Greenleaf Leavitt, Robert Keith Leavitt, and Constance Ruggli Leavitt Hanson. Thus it is called the Blazo-Leavitt house. Undoubtedly based on a handbook design by architect Thomas Eaton (also architect of the Taylor-Barry House in Kennebunk, Maine), the home is on the National Register of Historic Places.

The Blazo-Leavitt house has five large brick chimneys. The home also boasts elaborately carved and pillared entrances with leaded glass fans and sidelights, paneled doors, and small-paned windows. The main ell of the home was, built in 1812, the main part of the house being constructed five years later in 1817. The house faces south, and its western side faces Green Mountain, an isolated mountain in Effingham, New Hampshire and part of the foothills of the White Mountains.

William Blazo was son of Amos Blazo, who in turn was son of William Blazo of Bordeaux, France, who emigrated to America sometime before 1727, settling first in Greenland, New Hampshire, and later in Epsom. Amos Blazo is recorded in the History of Parsonsfield as having been North Parsonsfield's first settler, clearing the fields at "Blazo's Corner" in March 1778. Amos Blazo had five sons,

Robert T Blazo

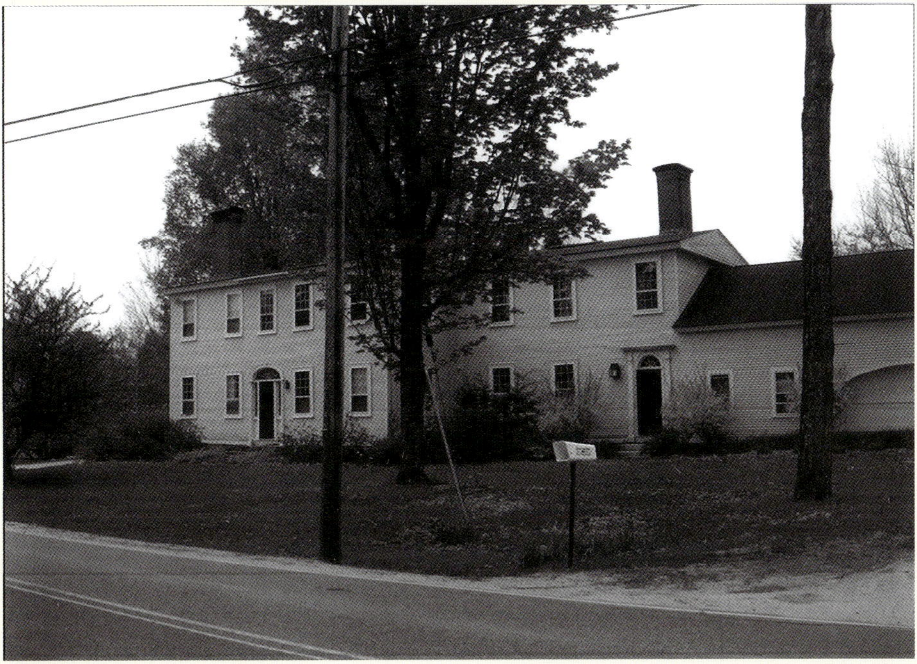

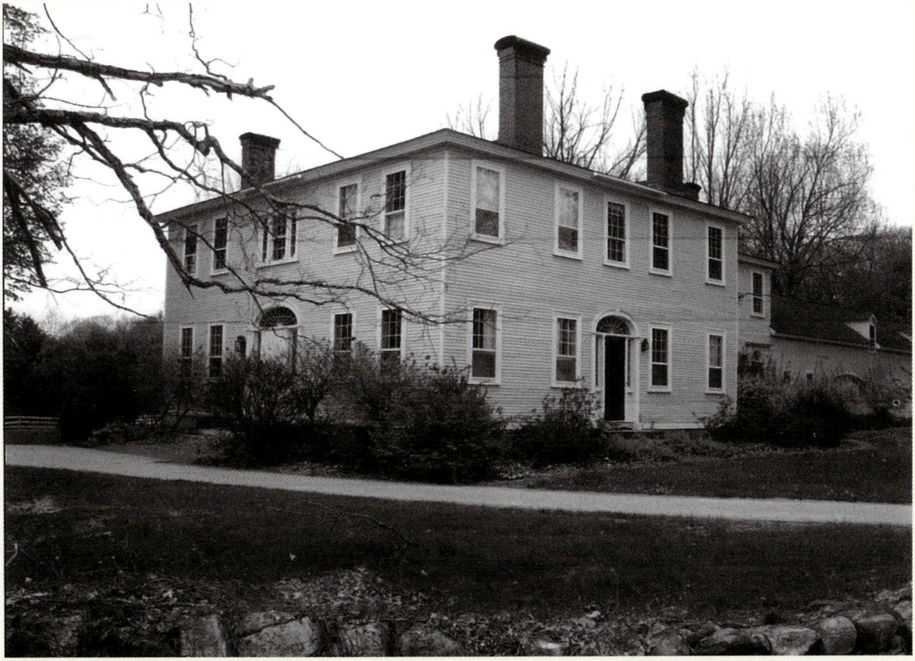

four of whom settled on nearby farms. It was Amos's son William who built the Blazo House, later selling it to his nephew, and Amos's grandson, Robert Tibbetts Blazo.

Robert Tibbetts Blazo had begun his career as a schoolmaster. One of his pupils was fifteen year old Mary Freeman of Sandwich, New Hampshire, who would become his bride eight years later. Before the marriage Robert Blazo practiced law for a time in Moultonborough, New Hampshire, but eventually the couple settled in Parsonsfield where Blazo practiced law, and was for many decades Justice of the Peace and Post Master. The couple had four children; Susan, Daniel, Charles and Emily. Descendants of Daniel still reside in the Daniel Blazo house directly across from the Blazo-Leavitt house at Blazo's Corner.

All four Blazo children attended Parsonsfield Seminary, to which their father had conveyed the land and helped establish. Here Susan Blazo met John Greenleaf Leavitt, a fellow student from Buckfield, Maine, who had come to Parsonsfield to prepare for Waterville College (today's Colby College). The couple married, and moved into the Blazo house with her parents; and they too took up residence in the house; they had one child, Maude Browne, who later became a portrait artist. Because Maude Browne was unable to have children, eventually ownership of the house came to the Leavitts and to their son Robert Greenleaf in 1942, Robert's wife Ida and their children, and grandchildren, and great grandchildren continued living in it every summer. Robert Greenleaf Leavitt's daughter, Constance Leavitt Hanson, with great regret sold the house in 1973.

RECORD OF _Clay, Robert Blazer_ .... DATE OF BIRTH .... ENTERED, MO. _September_ 19__

PREPARED AT .... SCHOOL, IN .... LEFT, MO. .... YR. 19__

RECEIVED TUFTS DEGREE OF _B.S._ IN _Mechanical Engineering_ .... AT COMMENCEMENT, 1920

RECORD OF COLLEGE WORK

ENTRANCE

ADMITTED

CREDITS

PRIMARY GROUP

- Elementary English
- Elem. Lang.
- Eng. Yr./Continental History
- Elementary Algebra
- Plane Geometry

SECONDARY GROUP   UNITS

SUMMARY IN TERM HOURS

MAJOR DEPARTMENT   NO

CONDITIONS & FAILURES   Only credits for completed work above this line; all failures, below, also first record of conditions. If condition is later removed, after credit as for following year, and in red.

Deceased 10/1/66

CONDITIONS

The mark (+) indicates credit by examination. (—) by certificate.

TUFTS COLLEGE   PRESCRIBED WORK COMPLETED, MO. .... YR. .... COMPUTED BY

COLLATERAL SUBJECTS

REQUIREMENT COMPLETED

Pa's transcript from Tufts College before and after the war.

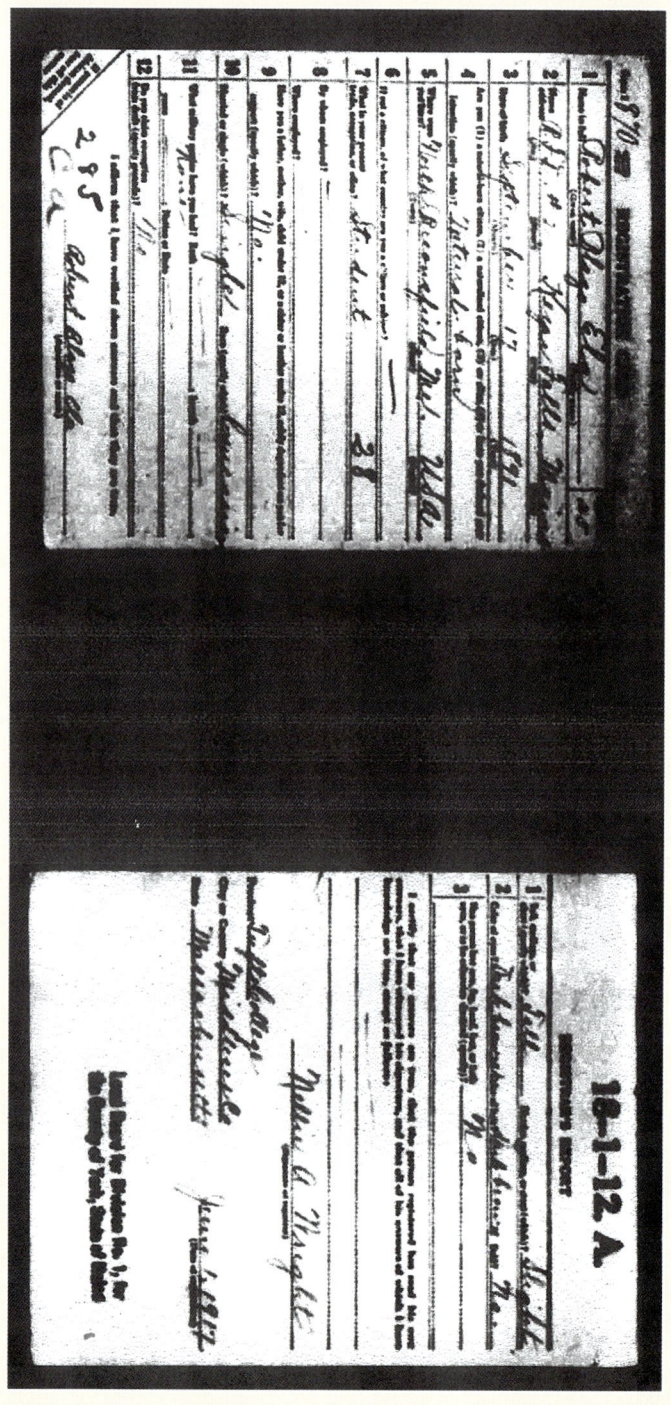

Pa's draft registration document filed June 1, 1917 at York, Maine.

Camp Deven's in Ayer, Mass., 1917.

Somewhere in France.
February 3, 1918.

Dear Wag:

I received your very interesting letter of December 20th, last week, and believe me, I was glad to hear from you. I also received a letter from E. B. Roberts on the same mail. You can't realize just how a fellow feels, when he is some three thousand or more miles from home and he gets some mail from the folks back there. I had quite a little spare time on board ship on the way across the pond, so I wrote letters to use up said time. As I wrote in my previous letter, we had a very quiet trip across. It became a little tiresome after a while, and when we pulled into —some French port, on the 14th day we were sure a glad bunch. We did not land until three days later and when we finally did set foot on solid ground, it certainly did feel good. We entrained about 10 a.m., and rode until 4 a.m. the next morning. The country through which we passed was very pretty. It was the middle of November and the fields were all green. The country was rather hilly and our little French engine had some job making some of the grades. The French engine is a good deal smaller than its American brother, but fairly powerful. The whistle reminds one of a peanut roaster in the States. The houses in France or rather the peasants' houses are of stone, usually white, one story and a half in height, and with either a tile or a thatched roof. Wood is a pretty scarce article over here. When we passed through some of the larger towns we saw bigger buildings, but not any that would come up to those at home.

When we arrived at our destination it was still dark. We got off the train and had to march about two miles to camp with our packs on our backs. It was so dark that we did not have a very good chance to see the town. When we finally reached camp it was still dark, and we were a pretty tired bunch. We were assigned to wooden barracks of the French type. These barracks are one story in height with dirt floors. Each barracks holds about 75 men. The first night that we were there we slept right close to Mother Earth. It was pretty hard, but we were so tired that we could have slept anywhere. One of the fellows went to sleep shortly after we got there, and when taps blew at 10 p.m., he started to get up, as he thought it was reveille. This camp, where we were first sent, was fixed up fine. We had a nice level drill ground and two large Y. M. C. A's. The only objectional feature was the damp weather; the reason for this being, I believe, its close proximity to the sea. The town there was a good sized one, but it being a seaport town, was nothing to boast about. There was another Y. M. C. A. down town. At all Y. M. C. A's. over here you can buy tobacco, candy, and toilet articles, and also procure writing paper.

We were at this camp until the last of November. We couldn't do our regular work at this place, as we did not have the equipment. Our work is map making and printing. You said in your letter that they were giving a course in map-making at college this year. All our work is done with the plane table. As I said before, we could not do our regular assigned work, so we did a little road work *a la* pick and shovel. We had one cheer that we used on every occasion, that went something like this:

Who are we? Who are we?
We are the pick of the countrie.
Picka da shove! Picka da shove!
Warp! Warp! Warp!

It was some strenuous work, and put a fellow in good shape, if he could stand it. We used a course rock foundation with a fill of small rocks and sand. After it was rolled down it made a very good road. In some very muddy places we had to use logs as the foundation.

We spent Thanksgiving at the above mentioned place. Our turkeys were delayed, so we had to be satisfied with chicken. They certainly did hand us a good feed. We had chicken, mashed potatoes, bread, coffee, butter (oleo.), PIE, and cranberry sauce. There was plenty of everything. We even had some chicken left over, which we had for supper. The day after Thanksgiving we got our October pay. We get paid in French currency and at first this is rather confusing to us foreigners, but soon you catch on to the system. You don't have any trouble in getting rid of it. On the first of December we got orders to pack up and get ready to move. At 4 p.m., we got on the train and were off again to "somewhere else in France." We travelled for two days and two nights, and about 5 p.m., on December 3rd, we pulled into this town. We got off the train and got a good look at our new home from the station. There was just about enough snow to cover the ground. (This disappeared after we had been here for awhile), and this made the walking, or rather marching, kind of slippery. The town here is situated on a hill overlooking the R. R. station in the valley below. The town, which is a very old one, is surrounded by a high wall. You enter the town by way of a drawbridge over a moat, which is now dry, (I mean the moat is dry) and through a gate in the wall. It was some climb up that hill to the town. The barracks here are located about fifteen minutes' walk outside of the centre of the town. We are quartered here in an old ————, I believe. The buildings are of stone, three stories in height, and all face on a parade ground. The floors in the building are of concrete and we sleep on bed ticks filled with straw and placed on said floor. It was pretty hard at first, but you get used to the hardships in this man's army. The

buildings are divided into rooms and each room will accommodate about 30 men. On the 3rd floor, the rooms run the entire width of the building with double French windows at either end. In each room there is a small stove in which we burn coal. The coal is not a very good quality but we manage to keep warm with it. We are very comfortably located here. The food is exceptionally good and plenty of it. You said in your letter that sugar was very scarce with you. We can buy sugar over at the commissary for seven and one-half cents a pound. How is that? You can also get tobacco and cigarettes over there. P. A. is seven and one-half cents a can (regular 10 cent size).

The weather here has been varied. We had our winter between the middle of December and the middle of January. We had some pretty cold weather during this period and plenty of snow. We were standing guard during that cold spell so that we derived the full benefit of it. Christmas it snowed all day, but they prepared a good feed for us at noon. This time the turkeys arrived O. K., and they were fine. We had roast turkey, mashed potatoes, bread, coffee, butter (oleo.), PIE, nuts and apples. We ate so much that.at supper time we did not feel hungry. In the evening the boys staged a show. It was very good. Our Christmas packages did not arrive until the 16th of January, but we celebrated just the same,—had Christmas all over. You see, our mail comes in bunches. We did not receive any until December 17th. Since then our mail has been coming about every two weeks. Our last lot arrived on January 28th, and your letter came on that date. I also had letters from "Kid" Ellis, Dempsey, and Roberts. It seemed good to hear from the boys.

This last week I have been putting my course in wood-working to good use. I have been working as a carpenter and expect to be on this job for some time. We had a lot of lumber come in from the U. S. the other day, also several chests of tools.

I think this place is going to be our permanent headquarters, as we are fixing up in a pretty elaborate fashion. We are not on the front, but back about —— miles I should judge. From every outward appearance you would not know that we are actually engaged in a war. We may see more of the real thing when the spring drive starts.

We have been having fine weather for the last two weeks. It has been nice and warm. Regular April weather. I hope we have some more just like the past two weeks. It is rather cool in the morning and at night, but during the day it is nice and warm. The other day I saw a rather odd and at the same time pretty sight. When we got up in the morning the trees were all covered with a heavy white frost. When the sun came out at noon it melted this frost enough just

Letter from Pa published in Tufts Weekly, continued on next page...

Letter from Pa published in Tufts Weekly,
...continued fron previous page

so that each tree had its own individual snow storm. The ground under the trees was all white. We have been having some very pretty sunsets this last two weeks.

Taking it all in, all, we are pretty well fixed here. In fact we are much better off than the boys at Camp Devens, except for the little stretch of 3,500 miles between us and home.

Well, Wag, I don't know just how soon we will be able to drop in and see you. It may be a year or more, but when we do get back we will have a lot to tell.

Remember me to all the boys around the Hill and also the professors. Write when you have any spare time and if you have any extra copies of the *Weekly* kicking around the house, just do them up and send them along. I will write again and let you know how I am getting along.

> Yours for Tufts, etc.,
> ROBERT B. ELA.

German Propaganda

"HOW TO STOP THE WAR"

DO YOUR PART TO PUT AN END TO THE WAR! Put an end to your part of it. Stop fighting! That's the simplest way. You can do it, you soldiers, just stop fighting and the war will end of its own accord. You are not fighting for anything, anyway. What does it matter to you who owns METZ or STRASSBURG; you never saw those towns nor knew the people in them. But there is a little town back home in little old UNITED STATES you would like to see and if you keep on fighting here in the hope of getting a look at those old German fortresses, you may never see home again.

The only way to stop the war is to stop fighting. That's easy. Just quit it and slip across no-man's land and join the bunch that's taking it easy there, waiting to be exchanged and taken home. There is no disgrace in that. That bunch of American prisoners will be welcomed just as warmly as you who stick it out in these infernal trenches. Get wise and get over the top.

Ther is nothing in the glory of keeping up the war. But think of the increasing taxes you will have to pay; the longer the war lasts the longer those taxes at home will be. Get wise and get over.

All the fine words about glory are tommy-rot. You haven't got any business fighting in France. You would better be fighting the money trust at home instead of fighting your fellow soldiers in gray over here where it doesn't really matter two sticks to you how the war goes.

Your country needs you; your family needs you; and you need your life for something better than being gassed, shot at, deafened by cannon shots and rendered physically unfit by the miserable life you must lead here.

The tales they tell you of the cruelties of the German prison camps are fairy tales. Of course, you may not like being a prisoner of war, but anything is better than this infernal place with no hope of escape except by being wounded, after which you will only be sent back for another hole in your body.

Wake up and stop the war! You can if you want to. Your government does not mean to stop the war for years to come, and the years are going to be long and dreary. You better come over the top while the going is good.

(German propaganda dropped from aeroplane on October 26th, 1918 in the Verdun sector)

German propaganda leaflet.

Still in Europe. May 1919

Camp Devens, Mass. _____ Aug. 11, 191 9
                    (Station)   (Date)

I CERTIFY that the men borne on this roll were discharged this date; that this roll exhibits the true pay status of each man borne herein on such date; that the entries opposite the name of each man are correct; that, unless otherwise noted in the remarks, each man borne herein is entitled to travel allowances and to foreign service

pay to include _____ 191 _ (date of arrival in U. S.),

and was last paid to include _____, 191 _

by _____, Quartermaster.

_____

I CERTIFY that I witnessed the payment of this roll and that prior to the signing of this certificate each man received the amount set opposite his name, with the exception of those men marked "Not paid."

_____
                                    Commanding Organization.

NOTE.—This certificate to be signed only on the copy of the pay roll which bears signatures of the men for payment in cash.

I CERTIFY that this roll is a true copy of the roll upon which payment, witnessed by me, was made, excepting as to the signatures in the receipt column and the certificate as to witnessing the payment thereof.

_____
                                    Commanding Organization.

_____ the roll not receipted, and which constitutes the quartermaster's retained voucher.

Voucher No. _____

John S. Barker, 1st Lt. Q. M. C.
(Name of quartermaster)

Paid, AUG. 22 1919, 191 _

FINAL PAYMENT ROLL

OF

_____
(Organization)

Discharged on _____, 191 _
                        (Date)

_____, 191 _
(Regiment.)   (Date)

APPROPRIATIONS

Pay, etc., of the Army, 1920 . . . . $ 2089.96
Pay, etc., of the Army, 1919 . . . . $ 213.70
General appropriations, Q. M. Corps, 1920 $ 122.10
Pay of the Army, Deposit Fund . . . .

AMOUNT, $ 2425.76

COLLECTIONS

Quartermaster . . . $
Post Exchange . . . $
Post Laundry . . . $ .20
Paid in Cash . . . $ 2399.32

TOTAL, $ 2425.76

ALLOTMENTS $ 100 no/100

2737

INSTRUCTIONS

1. The instructions governing the preparation of pay rolls and final statements should be followed as far as practicable in the preparation of final payment rolls.
2. All officers, noncommissioned officers, and others that may be concerned in the preparation of this roll are enjoined to exercise every care that it be made complete. It is not only the guide for immediate payment of the men interested, but, when filed in the Treasury Department, it will become the record to which reference will thereafter be made in the investigation and settlement of all claims or questions affecting the men whose names are borne on the roll, and their heirs, for the period covered by it.
3. Columns marked "Q. M." will be filled in by Quartermaster; columns marked "Pl. A." will be filled in by officer preparing roll.
4. In column "Partial pay previously received" should be entered the total amounts previously received as partial pay only when soldier is credited on this pay roll with payments in full from date to which last paid in full. When settlement is not made in full and soldier is credited with partial pay on this roll such amount will not be entered in this column.

Post Exchange collections hereon paid by checks on Treasurer of the United States dated _____, as follows:

Ft. _____, $ _____, No. _____
Ft. _____, $ _____, No. _____
Ft. _____, $ _____, No. _____

Post Laundry collections hereon paid by check on Treasurer of the United States dated _____, as follows:

Ft. _____, $ _____, No. _____
Ft. _____, $ _____, No. _____
Ft. _____, $ _____, No. _____

WAR DEPARTMENT
Form No. 371
Approved by Comptroller of Treasury
November 21, 1918.

3—0631

U.S. Army Financial Discharge Documents.

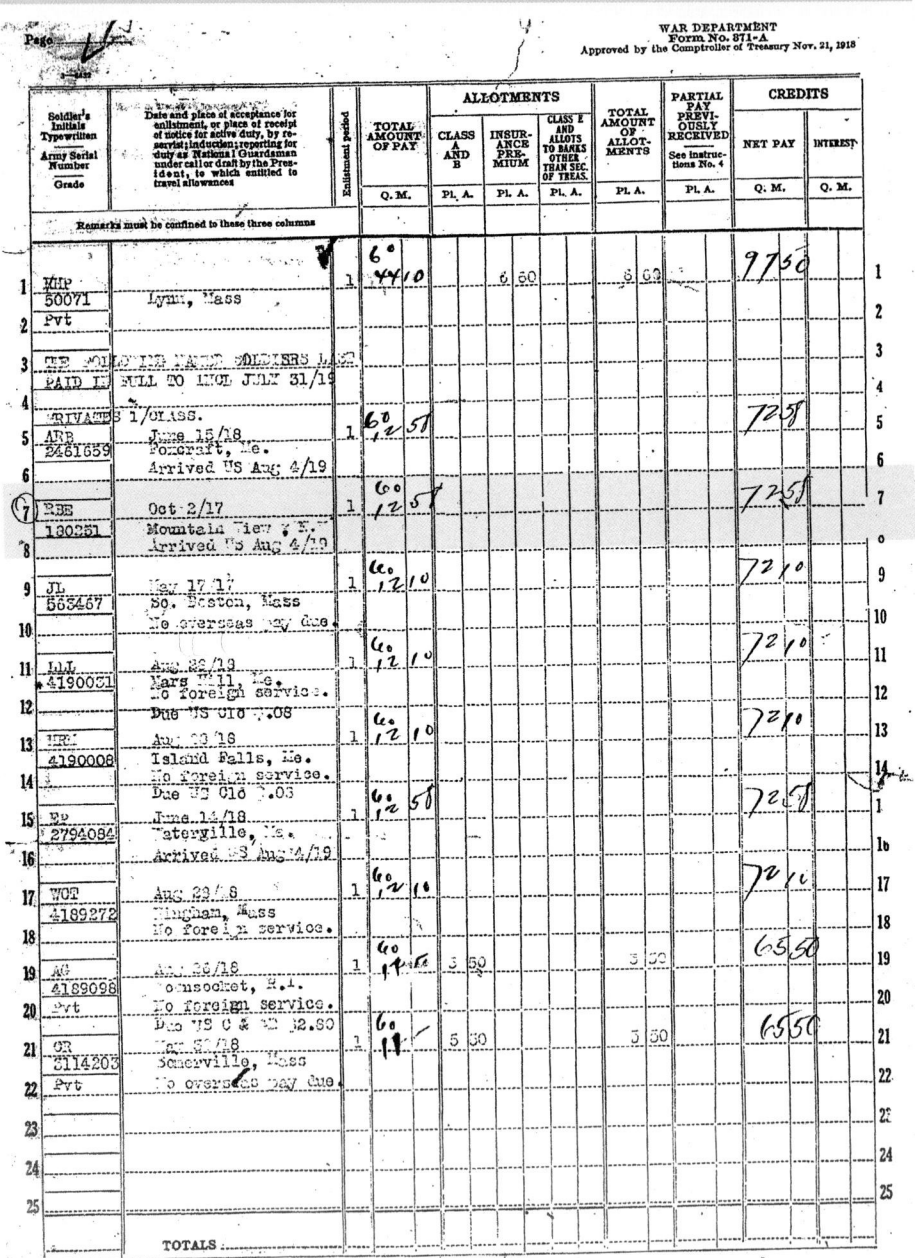

WAR DEPARTMENT
Form No. 371-A
Approved by the Comptroller of Treasury Nov. 21, 1918

Soldier's Initials Typewritten Army Serial Number Grade	Date and place of acceptance for enlistment, or place of receipt of notice for active duty, by reservice, induction, reporting for duty as National Guardsman under call or draft by the President, to which entitled to travel allowances	Enlistment period	TOTAL AMOUNT OF PAY	ALLOTMENTS			TOTAL AMOUNT OF ALLOTMENTS	PARTIAL PAY PREVIOUSLY RECEIVED See instructions No. 4	CREDITS		
				CLASS A AND B	INSURANCE PREMIUM	CLASS E AND ALLOTS TO BANKS OTHER THAN SEC. OF TREAS.			NET PAY	INTEREST	
Remarks must be confined to these three columns			Q. M.	Pl. A.	Pl. A.	Pl. A.	Pl. A.	Pl. A.	Q. M.	Q. M.	
1 MIP 50071 Pvt	Lynn, Mass	1	6° 44 10		6 50		6 50		97 50		1 2
3 THE MONEY DUE THESE SOLDIERS WAS PAID IN FULL TO INCL JULY 31/19											3 4
5 PRIVATES 1/CLASS. ARB 2461659	June 15/18 Foxcroft, Me. Arrived US Aug 4/19	1	6° 12 51						72 51		5 6
7 RBE 130251	Oct 2/17 Mountain View, N.Y. Arrived US Aug 4/19	1	6° 12 51						72 51		8
9 JL 563467	May 17/17 So. Boston, Mass No overseas pay due	1	6° 12 10						72 10		10
11 LLL 4190031	Aug 26/18 Mars Hill, Me. No foreign service. Due US O16 0.08	1	6° 12 10						72 10		12
13 HRI 4190008	Aug 23/18 Island Falls, Me. No foreign service. Due US O16 0.03	1	6° 12 10						72 10		14
15 RP 2794084	June 14/18 Waterville, Me. Arrived US Aug 4/19	1	6° 12 51						72 51		16
17 WOT 4189272	Aug 22/18 Hingham, Mass No foreign service.	1	6° 12 10						72 10		18
19 AG 4189098 Pvt	Aug 26/18 Woonsocket, R.I. No foreign service. Due US C & M 32.80	1	6° 14 50	5 50			5 50		65 50		20
21 OR 3114203 Pvt	May 3/18 Somerville, Mass No overseas pay due	1	6° 14 50	5 50			5 50		65 50		22
23											23
24											24
25											25
TOTALS											

Pa's discharge is recorded on line 7.

CREDITS—Continued			TOTAL CREDITS	COLLECTIONS			TOTAL AMOUNT OF STOPPAGES	BALANCE PAID TO SOLDIER	Received Payment in Cash of (Name of Quartermaster)
DEPOSITS	CLOTHING	TRAVEL PAY		POST EXCHANGE	POST LAUNDRY	OTHER STOPPAGES			Name, Grade, and Organization
Pl. A.	Pl. A.	Q. M.	Q. M.	Pl. A.	Pl. A.	Q. M.	Q. M.	Q. M.	Soldier's name will be typewritten, surname first, and he will sign above it in same space, Christian name first.
		2 40	99 90					99 90	*René H. Pelletier* Pelletier, Rene H. ✓
		13 —	85 58					85 58	*Albert R Beane* Beane, Albert R ✓
		7 35	79 93					79 93	*Robert B. Ela* Ela, Robert B
		1	90 74					74 —	*John Lou* Lou, John
		21 40	93 50			08	08	93 42	*Lester L Bains* Bains, Lester L ✓
		18 20	90 30			08	08	90 22	*Harvey R Morrow* Morrow, Harvey R
		10 25	82 83					82 83	*Edward Pooler* Pooler, Edward
		2 75	74 85	80			80	74 05	*Chester C Thayer* Thayer, Chester C ✓
		2 65	68 15	40	2 80		3 20	64 95	*Alfred Gagnon* Gagnon, Alfred
		1 75	67 25					67 25	*Charles Reynolds* Reynolds, Charles
								TOTALS	

Reading List

Bailey, Temple. *Contrary Mary*. London: Hurst and Blackett Ltd. 1914.

Daudet, Alphonse. *La Belle Nivernaise*. Trans: Robert Routledge. London: J. Fisher Unwin, 1892.

Ela, Rev. David Hough, D.D. *Genealogy of the Ela Family: Descendants of Israel Ela of Haverill, Mass.* Manchester, Connecticut, USA: Elwood S. Ela, Printer, 1896. Reprint by Charleston, South Carolina, USA: Nabu Press, 2014.

Janis, Elsie. *The Big Show: My Six Months with the American Expeditionary Forces*. New York: Cosmopolitan Book Corporation, 1919. Reprint by London: Forgotten Books, 2017.

Leacock, Stephen. *Nonsense Novels*. London: John Lane The Bodley Head, 1921.

London, Jack. *The Valley of the Moon*. New York: Macmillan Company, 1913. Reprint by Whitefish, Montana, USA: Kessinger Publishing, 2016.

Robinson, William. *Forging the Sword: The Story of Camp Devens, New England's Army Cantonment*. Concord, New Hampshire, USA: The Rumford Press, 1920. Reprint by: South Yarra, Victoria, Australia: Leopold Classic Library, 2017.

Afterword

I must apologise for being unable to identify with certainty the folks who appear in the photos so carefully kept in the diary. I could guess which soldier is Pa or which of the lovely young ladies turns out to be my Nana but what would be the point? I must content myself with the knowledge that the photos she sent and he treasured served to keep their love alive throughout a long separation under uncertain and perilous circumstances.

There are many people without whom I could not have prepared this little book. Thanks must go to:
...my sister Patricia Rose for securing photos and information from other members of the family.
...my hitherto unknown second cousin Jean Stanley, the Ela and Blazo family historian from Maine, for genealogical information (and surprises), photos, and enthusiasm.
...Sylvia Wilson, President of the Parsonsfield Porter Historical Society for material on distant Blazo relatives and the Blazo-Leavitt House. She also put me in touch with Jean Stanley.
...Kara Fossey, Executive Director of the Fort Devens Museum in Ayer, Massachusetts for facts and photos of Camp Devens.
...the very helpful staff at the Tufts University Archives for providing a copy of my grandad's transcript and a copy of the letter he sent to the Tufts Club from France.
...Tom Cann, Jill Cann and the whole crew at TUCANNbooks for giving me, a complete novice in the world of publishing, sound advice and good guidance. I must also salute their unfailing patience with me and my seemingly endless pages of corrections.

And most of all... to my beloved husband Pip for everything.